The Voyageur and Other Poems

William Henry Drummond

Contents

THE VOYAGEUR
AND OTHER POEMS

BY

William Henry Drummond

TO

WILLIAM HENRY PARKER

LAC LA PECHE

Philosopher of many parts,

Beloved of all true honest hearts,

A man who laughs at every ill,

Because "there's corn in Egypt still."

The Voyageur and Other Poems

The Voyageur

Dere's somet'ing stirrin' ma blood tonight,
   On de night of de young new year,
Wile de camp is warm an' de fire is bright,
   An' de bottle is close at han'--
Out on de reever de nort' win' blow,
Down on de valley is pile de snow,

But w'at do we care so long we know
   We 're safe on de log cabane?

Drink to de healt' of your wife an' girl,
   Anoder wan for your frien',
Den geev' me a chance, for on all de worl'
   I 've not many frien' to spare--
I 'm born, w'ere de mountain scrape de sky,
An' bone of ma fader an' moder lie,
So I fill de glass an' I raise it high
   An' drink to de Voyageur.

For dis is de night of de jour de l'an,[1]
   W'en de man of de Grand Nor' Wes'
T'ink of hees home on de St. Laurent,
   An' frien' he may never see--
Gone he is now, an' de beeg canoe
No more you 'll see wit' de red-shirt crew,
But long as he leev' he was alway true,
   So we 'll drink to hees memory.

Ax' heem de nort' win' w'at he see
   Of de Voyageur long ago,
An' he 'll say to you w'at he say to me,
   So lissen hees story well--
"I see de track of hees botte sau-vage[2]
On many a hill an' long portage
Far far away from hees own vill-age
   An' soun' of de parish bell--

"I never can play on de Hudson Bay

Or mountain dat lie between
But I meet heem singin' hees lonely way
    De happies' man I know--
I cool hees face as he 's sleepin' dere
Under de star of de Red Riviere,
An' off on de home of de great w'ite bear,
    I 'm seein' hees dog traineau.[3]

"De woman an' chil'ren 's runnin' out
    On de wigwam of de Cree--
De leetle papoose dey laugh an' shout
    W'en de soun' of hees voice dey hear--
De oldes' warrior of de Sioux
Kill hese'f dancin' de w'ole night t'roo,
An de Blackfoot girl remember too
    De ole tam Voyageur.

"De blaze of hees camp on de snow I see,
    An' I lissen hees 'En Roulant'
On de lan' w'ere de reindeer travel free,
    Ringin' out strong an' clear--
Offen de grey wolf sit before
De light is come from hees open door,
An' caribou foller along de shore
    De song of de Voyageur.

"If he only kip goin', de red ceinture,[4]
    I 'd see it upon de Pole
Some mornin' I 'm startin' upon de tour
    For blowin' de worl' aroun'--
But w'erever he sail an' w'erever he ride,
De trail is long an' de trail is wide,
An' city an' town on ev'ry side

Can tell of hees campin' groun'."

So dat 's 'de reason I drink to-night
    To de man of de Grand Nor' Wes',
For hees heart was young, an' hees heart was light
    So long as he 's leevin' dere--
I 'm proud of de sam' blood in my vein
I 'm a son of de Nort' Win' wance again--
So we 'll fill her up till de bottle 's drain
    An' drink to de Voyageur.

[1] New Year's day.

[2] Indian boot.

[3] Dog-sleigh.

[4] Canadian sash.

BRUNO THE HUNTER

You never hear tell, Marie, ma femme,
    Of Bruno de hunter man,
Wit' hees wild dogs chasin' de moose an' deer,
Every day on de long, long year,
Off on de hillside far an' near,
    An' down on de beeg savane?

Not'ing can leev' on de woods, Marie,
    W'en Bruno is on de track,
An' young caribou, an' leetle red doe
Wit' baby to come on de spring, dey know
De pity dey get w'en hees bugle blow
    An' de black dogs answer back.

No bird on de branch can finish hees song,
    De squirrel no longer play--
De leaf on de maple don't need to wait
Till fros' of October is at de gate
'Fore de blood drops come: an' de fox sleeps late
    W'en Bruno is pass dat way.

So de devil ketch heem of course at las'
    Dat 's w'at de ole folk say,
An' spik to heem, "Bruno, w'at for you kill
De moose an' caribou of de hill
An' fill de woods wit' deir blood until
    You could run a mill night an' day?"

"Mebbe you lak to be moose youse'f,
    An' see how de hunter go,
So I 'll change your dogs into loup garou,[1]
An' wance on de year dey 'll be chasin' you--
An' res' of de tam w'en de sport is troo,
    You 'll pass wit' me down below."

An' dis is de night of de year, Marie,
    Bruno de hunter wake:
Soon as de great beeg tonder cloud
Up on de mountain 's roarin' loud--
He 'll come from hees grave w'ere de pine tree crowd
    De shore of de leetle lake.

You see de lightning zig, zig, Marie,
    Spittin' lak' loup cervier,[2]
Ketch on de trap? Oh! it won't be long
Till mebbe you lissen anoder song,
For de sky is dark an' de win' is strong,
    An' de chase is n't far away.

W'y shiver so moche, Marie, ma femme,
    For de log is burnin' bright?
Ah! dere she's goin', "Hulloo! Hulloo!"
An' oh! how de tonder is roarin' too!
But it can't drown de cry of de loup garou
    On Bruno de hunter's night.

Over de mountain an' t'roo de swamp,
    Don't matter how far or near,
Every place hees moccasin know

Bruno de hunter he 's got to go
'Fore de grave on de leetle lake below
   Close up for anoder year.

But dey say de ole feller watch all night,
   So you need n't be scare, Marie,
For he 'll never stir from de rocky cave
W'ere door only open beneat' de wave,
Till Bruno come back to hees lonely grave--
   An' de devil he turn de key.

Dat 's way for punish de hunter man
   W'en murder is on hees min'--
So he better stop w'ile de work is new,
Or mebbe de devil will ketch heem too,
An' chase heem aroun' wit' de loup garou
   Gallopin' close behin'.

[1] Were wolf.

[2] Lynx.

PRIDE

Ma fader he spik to me long ago,
   "Alphonse, it is better go leetle slow,
Don't put on de style if you can't afford,

But satisfy be wit' your bed an' board.
De bear wit' hees head too high alway,
    Know not'ing at all till de trap go smash.
An' mooshrat dat 's swimmin' so proud to-day
    Very often to-morrow is on de hash." [1]

Edouard de Seven of Angleterre,
    An' few oder place beside,
He 's got de horse an' de carriage dere
    W'enever he want to ride.
Wit' sojer in front to clear de way,
Sojer behin' all dress so gay,
Ev'rywan makin' de grand salaam,
An' plaintee o' ban' playin' all de tam

Edouard de Seven of Angleterre,
    All he has got to do,
W'en he 's crossin' de sea, don't matter w'ere,
    Is call for de ship an' crew.
Den hois' de anchor from down below,
Vive le Roi! an' away she go,
An' flag overhead, w'en dey see dat sight
W'ere is de nation don't be polite?

An' dere 's de boss of United State,
    An' w'at dey call Philippine--
De Yankee t'ink he was somet'ing great,
    An' beeg as de king or queen--
So dey geev' heem a house near touch de sky,
An' paint it so w'ite it was blin' de eye
An' long as he 's dere beginnin' to en',
Don't cos' heem not'ing for treat hees frien'.

So dere 's two feller, Edouard de King
    An' Teddy Roos-vel' also,
No wonder dey 're proud, for dey got few t'ing
    Was helpin' dem mak' de show--
But oh! ma Gosh! w'en you talk of pride
An' w'at dey call style, an' puttin' on side,
W'ere is de man can go before
De pig-sticker champion of Ste. Flore?

Use to be nice man too, dey say,
    Jeremie Bonami,
Talk wit' hees frien' in a frien'ly way
    Sam' as you'se'f an' me--
Of course it 's purty beeg job he got,
An' no wan expec' heem talk a lot,
But still would n't hurt very moche, I 'm sure,
If wance in a w'ile he 'd say, "Bonjour."

Yi! Yi! to see heem come down de hill
    Some mornin' upon de fall,
W'en de pig is fat an' ready to kill,
    He don't know hees frien' at all--
Look at hees face an' it seem to say,
"Important duty I got to-day,
Killin' de pig on de contree side,--
Is n't dat some reason for leetle pride?"

Lissen de small boy how dey shout
    W'en Jeremie 's marchin' t'roo
De market place wit' hees cane feex out
    Wit' ribbon red, w'ite an' blue--
An' den he jomp on de butcher's block,
An' affer de crowd is stop deir talk,

An' leetle boy holler no more "Hooray,"
Dis is de word Jeremie he say--

"I 'm de only man on de w'ole Ste. Flore
    Can kill heem de pig jus' right,
Please t'ink of dat, an' furdermore
    Don't matter it 's day or night,
Can do it less tam, five dollar I bet,
Dan any pig-sticker you can get
From de w'ole of de worl', to w'ere I leev'--
Will somebody help to roll up ma sleeve?

"Some feller challenge jus' here an' dere,
    An' more on deir own contree,
But me--I challenge dem ev'ryw'ere
    All over de worl'--sapree!
To geev' dem a chance, for dere might be some
    Beeg feller, for all I know,
But if dey 're ready, wall! let dem come,
    An' me--I 'm geevin' dem plaintee show."

Challenge lak dat twenty year or more
    He 's makin' it ev'ry fall,
But never a pig-sticker come Ste. Flore
    'Cos Jeremie scare dem all--
No wonder it 's makin' heem feel so proud,
    Even Emperor Germanie
Can't put on de style or talk more loud
    Dan Jeremie Bonami.

But Jeremie's day can't las' alway,
    An' so he commence to go
W'en he jomp on de block again an' say

To de crowd stan'nin' dere below,
"Lissen, ma frien', to de word I spik,
For I 'm tire of de challenge until I 'm sick,
Can't say, but mebbe I 'll talk no more
For glory an' honor of ole Ste. Flore.

"I got some trouble aroun' ma place
    Wit' ma nice leetle girl Rosine,
An' I see w'en I 'm lookin' on all de face,
    You 're knowin' jus' w'at I mean--
Very easy to talk, but w'en dey come
For seein' her twenty young man ba Gum!
I tole you ma frien', it was purty tough,
'Sides wan chance in twenty is not enough--

"Now lissen to me, all you young man
    Is wantin' ma girl Rosine--
I offer a chance an' you 'll understan'
    It 's bes' you was never seen--
Tree minute start I 'll geev'--no more--
An' if any young feller upon Ste. Flore
Can beat me stickin' de pig nex' fall,
Let heem marry ma girl Rosine--dat 's all."

All right--an' very nex' week he start,
    De smartes' boy of de lot--
An' he 's lovin' Rosine wit' all hees heart,
    De young Adelard Marcotte--
Don't say very moche about w'ere he go,
But I t'ink mese'f it was Buffalo--
An' plaintee more place on de State dat's beeg
W'ere he don't do not'ing but stick de pig.

So of course he 's pickin' de fancy trick
    An' ev'ryt'ing else dey got--
Work over tam--but he got homesick
    De young Adelard Marcotte
Jus' about tam w'en de fall come along---
So den he wissle hees leetle song
An' buy tiquette for de ole Ste. Flore,
An' back on de village he come some more.

Ho! Ho! ma Jeremie Bonami,
    Get ready you'se'f to-day,
For you got beeg job you was never see
    Will tak' all your breat' away--
"Come on! come on!" dey be shoutin' loud,
De Bishop hese'f could n't draw de crowd
Of folk on de parish for mile aroun',
Till dey could n't fin' place upon de groun'.

Hi! Hi! Jeremie, you may sweat an' swear,
    Your tam is arrive at las'--
Dere 's no use pullin' out all your hair
    Or drinkin' de w'isky glass--
Spit on your han' or hitch de pants--
You 'll never have anyt'ing lak a chance,
Hooraw! Hooraw! let her go wance more,
An' Adelard 's champion of all Ste. Flore!

"Away on de pump!" de crowd is yell,
    "No use for heem goin' die."
Dey nearly drown Jeremie on de well
    But he 's comin' roun' bimeby
Rosine dat 's laughin' away all day
Is startin' to cry, an' den she say--

"O fader dear, won't you geev' me kiss
For I never s'pose it would come to dis?

"Don't blame de boy over dere, 't was me
    Dat sen' away Adelard--
He 's sorry for beat you, I 'm sure, ba oui,
    An' dat 's w'at I 'm cryin' for--
'Cos it 's all ma fault you was lick to-day,
Don't care w'at anywan else can say--
But remember too, an' you 'll not forget
De championship 's still on de familee yet."
    An' de ole man smile.

[1] Old proverb of Ste. Flore.

Dieudonne

(GOD-GIVEN)

If I sole ma ole blind trotter for fifty dollar cash
    Or win de beeges' prize on lotterie,
If some good frien' die an' lef' me fines' house on St. Eustache,
    You t'ink I feel more happy dan I be?

No, sir! An' I can tole you, if you never know before,
    W'y de kettle on de stove mak' such a fuss,

Wy de robin stop hees singin' an' come peekin' t'roo de door
   For learn about de nice t'ing 's come to us--

An' w'en he see de baby lyin' dere upon de bed
   Lak leetle Son of Mary on de ole tam long ago--
Wit' de sunshine an' de shadder makin' ring aroun' hees head,
   No wonder M'sieu Robin wissle low.

An' we can't help feelin' glad too, so we call heem Dieudonne;
   An' he never cry, dat baby, w'en he 's chrissen by de pries'
All de sam' I bet you dollar he 'll waken up some day,
   An' be as bad as leetle boy Bateese.

THE DEVIL

Along de road from Bord a Plouffe
   To Kaz-a-baz-u-a
W'ere poplar trees lak sojers stan',
An' all de lan' is pleasan' lan',
In off de road dere leev's a man
   Call Louis Desjardins.

An' Louis, w'en he firse begin
   To work hees leetle place,
He work so hard de neighbors say,
"Unless he tak's de easy way
Dat feller 's sure to die some day,
   We see it on hees face."

'T was lak a swamp, de farm he got,
   De water ev'ryw'ere--
Might drain her off as tight as a drum.
An' back dat water is boun' to come
In less 'n a day or two--ba Gum!
   'T would mak' de angel swear.

So Louis t'ink of de bimeby,
   If he leev' so long as dat,
W'en he 's ole an' blin' an' mebbe deaf,
All alone on de house hese'f,
No frien', no money, no not'ing lef',
   An' poor--can't kip a cat.

So wan of de night on winter tam,
   W'en Louis is on hees bed,
He say out loud lak a crazy man,
"I 'm sick of tryin' to clear dis lan',
Work any harder I can't stan',
   Or it will kill me dead.

"Now if de devil would show hese'f
   An' say to me, 'Tiens! Louis!
Hard tam an' work she 's at an' en',
You 'll leev' lak a Grand Seigneur ma frien',
If only you 'll be ready w'en
   I want you to come wit' me.'

"I 'd say, 'Yass, yass--'maudit! w'at 's dat?'
   An' he see de devil dere--
Brimstone, ev'ryt'ing bad dat smell,
You know right away he 's come from--well,

De place I never was care to tell--
    An' wearin' hees long black hair,

Lak election man, de kin' I mean
    You see aroun' church door,
Spreadin' hese'f on great beeg speech
'Bout poor man 's goin' some day be reech,
But dat 's w'ere it alway come de heetch,
    For poor man 's alway poor.

De only diff'rence--me--I see
    'Tween devil an' long-hair man
It 's hard to say, but I know it 's true,
W'en devil promise a t'ing to do
Dere 's no mistak', he kip it too--
    I hope you understan'.

So de devil spik, "You 're not content,
    An' want to be reech, Louis--
All right, you 'll have plaintee, never fear,
No wan can beat you far an' near,
An' I 'll leave you alone for t'orty year,
    An' den you will come wit' me.

"Be careful now--it 's beeg contrac',
    So mebbe it 's bes' go slow;
For me--de promise I mak' to you
Is good as de bank Riviere du Loup
For you--w'enever de tam is due,
    Ba tonder! you got to go."

Louis try hard to tak' hees tam
    But w'en he see de fall

Comin' along in a week or so,
All aroun' heem de rain an' snow
An' pork on de bar'l runnin' low,
    He don't feel good at all.

An' w'en he t'ink of de swampy farm
    An' gettin' up winter night,
Watchin' de stove if de win' get higher
For fear de chimley go on fire,
It's makin' poor Louis feel so tire
    He tell de devil, "All right."

"Correct," dat feller say right away,
    "I 'll only say, Au revoir,"
An' out of de winder he 's goin' pouf!
Beeg nose, long hair, short tail, an' hoof,
Off on de road to Bord a Plouffe
    Crossin' de reever dere.

W'en Louis get up nex' day, ma frien',
    Dere 's lot of devil sign--
Bar'l o' pork an' keg o' rye,
Bag o' potato ten foot high,
Pile o' wood nearly touch de sky,
    Was some o' de t'ing he fin'.

Suit o' clothes would have cos' a lot
    An' ev'ryt'ing I dunno,
Trotter horse w'en he want to ride
Eatin' away on de barn outside,
Stan' all day if he 's never tied,
    An' watch an' chain also.

An' swamp dat's bodder heem many tam,
    W'ere is dat swamp to-day?
Don't care if you 're huntin' up an' down
You won't fin' not'ing but medder groun',
An' affer de summer come aroun'
    W'ere can you see such hay?

Wall! de year go by, an' Louis leev'
    Widout no work to do,
Rise w'en he lak on winter day,
Fin' all de snow is clear away,
No fuss, no not'ing, dere 's de sleigh
    An' trotter waitin' too.

W'en t'orty year is nearly t'roo
    An' devil 's not come back
'Course Louis say, 'Wall! he forget
Or t'ink de tam 's not finish yet;
I 'll tak' ma chance an' never fret,"
    But dat 's w'ere he mak' mistak'.

For on a dark an' stormy night
    W'en Louis is sittin' dere,
After he fassen up de door
De devil come as he come before,
Lookin' de sam' only leetle more,
    For takin' heem--you know w'ere.

"Asseyez vous, sit down, ma frien',
    Bad night be on de road;
You come long way an' should be tire--
Jus' wait an' mebbe I feex de fire--
Tak' off your clothes for mak' dem drier,

Dey mus' be heavy load."

Dat 's how poor Louis Desjardins
    Talk to de devil, sir--
Den say, "Try leetle w'isky blanc,
Dey 're makin' it back on St. Laurent--
It 's good for night dat 's cole an' raw,"
    But devil never stir,

Until he smell de smell dat come
    W'en Louis mak' it hot
Wit' sugar, spice, an' ev'ryt'ing.
Enough to mak' a man's head sing--
For winter, summer, fall an' spring--
    It 's very bes' t'ing we got.

An' so de devil can't refuse
    To try de w'isky blanc,
An' say, "I 'm tryin' many drink,
An' dis is de fines' I don't t'ink,
De firse, ba tonder! mak' me wink--
    Hooraw, pour Canadaw!"

"Merci--non, non--I tak' no more,"
    De devil say at las',
"For tam is up wit' you, Louis,
So come along, ma frien', wit' me,
So many star I 'm sure I see,
    De storm she mus' be pas'."

"No hurry--wait a minute, please,"
    Say Louis Desjardins,
"We 'll have a smoke before we 're t'roo,

'T will never hurt mese'f or you
To try a pipe, or mebbe two,
   Of tabac Canayen." [1]

"Wan pipe is all I want for me--
   We 'll finish our smoke downstair,"
De devil say, an' it was enough,
For w'en he tak' de very firse puff
He holler out, "Maudit! w'at stuff!
   Fresh air! fresh air!! fresh air!!!"

An' oh! he was never sick before
   Till he smoke tabac Bruneau--
Can't walk or fly, but he want fresh air,
So Louis put heem on rockin' chair
An' t'row heem off on de road out dere--
   An' tole heem go below.

An' he shut de door an' fill de place
   Wit' tabac Canayen,
An' never come out, an' dat 's a fac'--
But smoke away till hees face is black--
So dat 's w'y de devil don't come back
   For Louis Desjardins.

An' dere he 's yet, an' dere he 'll stay--
   So weech of de two 'll win
Can't say for dat--it 's kin' of a doubt,
For Louis, de pipe never leave hees mout',
An' night or day can't ketch heem out,
   An' devil 's too scare go in.

[1] Canadian tobacco.

The Family Laramie

Hssh! look at ba-bee on de leetle blue chair,
    W'at you t'ink he 's tryin' to do?
Wit' pole on de han' lak de lumberman,
    A-shovin' along canoe.
Dere 's purty strong current behin' de stove,
    W'ere it 's passin' de chimley-stone,
But he 'll come roun' yet, if he don't upset,
    So long he was lef' alone.

Dat 's way ev'ry boy on de house begin
    No sooner he 's twelve mont' ole;
He 'll play canoe up an' down de Soo
    An' paddle an' push de pole,
Den haul de log all about de place,
    Till dey 're fillin' up mos' de room,
An' say it 's all right, for de storm las' night
    Was carry away de boom.

Mebbe you see heem, de young loon bird,
    Wit' half of de shell hangin' on,
Tak' hees firse slide to de water side,
    An' off on de lake he 's gone.
Out of de cradle dey 're goin' sam' way
    On reever an' lake an' sea;

For born to de trade, dat 's how dey 're made,
    De familee Laramie.

An' de reever she 's lyin' so handy dere
    On foot of de hill below,
Dancin' along an' singin' de song
    As away to de sea she go,
No wonder I never can lak dat song,
    For soon it is comin', w'en
Dey 'll lissen de call, leetle Pierre an' Paul,
    An' w'ere will de moder be den?

She 'll sit by de shore w'en de evenin's come,
    An' spik to de reever too:
"O reever, you know how dey love you so,
    Since ever dey 're seein' you,
For sake of dat love bring de leetle boy home
    Once more to de moder's knee."
An' mebbe de prayer I be makin' dere
    Will help bring dem back to me.

Yankee Families

You s'pose God love de Yankee
    An' de Yankee woman too,
Lak he love de folk at home on Canadaw?
    I dunno--'cos if he do,
W'at 's de reason he don't geev' dem familee

Is dere anybody hangin' roun' can answer me
Wile I wait an' smoke dis pipe of good tabac?

An' now I 'll tole you somet'ing
   Mebbe help you bimeby,
An' dere 's no mistak' it 's w'at dey call sure sign--
   W'en you miss de baby's cry
As you 're goin' mak' some visit on de State
Dat 's enough--you need n't ax if de train 's on tam or late,
You can bet you 're on de Yankee side de line.

Unless dere 's oder folk dere,
   Mebbe wan or two or t'ree,
Canayen is comin' workin' on de State--
   Den you see petite Marie
Leetle Joe an' Angelique, Hormisdas an' Dieudonne,
But you can't tole half de nam'--it don't matter any way--
'Sides de fader he don't t'ink it's not'ing great.

De moder, you can see her
   An' she got de basket dere
Wit' de fine t'ing for de chil'ren nice an' slick--
   For dey can't get fat on air--
Cucumber, milk, an' onion, some leetle cake also
De ole gran'moder 's makin' on de farm few days ago--
W'at 's use buy dollar dinner mak' dem sick?

But look de Yankee woman
   Wit' de book upon her han',
Readin', readin', an' her husban', he can't get
   Any chance at all, poor man,
For sit down, de way de seat's all pile up wit' magazine--
De t'ing lak dat on Canadaw is never, never seen.

Would n't she be better wit' some chil'ren? Wall! you bet!

No wonder dey was bringin'
      For helpin' dem along
So many kin' of feller I dunno--
      Chinee washee from Kong Kong
An' w'at dey call Da-go, was work for dollar a day,
But w'en dey mak' some money, off dey 're goin', right away--
Dat 's de reason dey was get de nam' Da-go.

Of course so long dey 're comin'
      From ev'ry place dey can,
Not knowin' moche, dere 's not'ing fuss about
      Only boss de stranger man--
But now dem gang of feller dat 's come across de sea--
He 's gettin' leetle smarter, an' he got de familee--
So Uncle Sam mus' purty soon look out.

I wonder he don't know it--
      It 's funny he don't see
Dere 's somet'ing else dan money day an' night--
      Non--he 'll work hese'f cra-zee,
Den travel roun' de worl', an' use de money too--
De King hese'f can't spen' lak de Yankee man is do--
But w'ere 's de leetle chil'ren? dat's not right!

W'at 's use of all de money
      If dere ain't some boy an' girl
Mak' it pleasan' for de Yankee an' hees wife
      W'en dey travel on de worl'?
For me an' Eugenie dere 's not'ing we lak bes'
Dan gader up de chil'ren an' get dem nicely dress--
W'y it 's more dan half de pleasure of our life.

I love de Yankee woman
    An' de Yankee man also,
An' mebbe dey 'll be wiser bimeby--
    But I lak dem all to know
If dey want to kip deir own, let dem raise de familee--
An' den dey 'll boss de contree from de mountain to de sea,
For dey 're smart enough to do it if dey try.

The Last Portage

I'm sleepin' las' night w'en I dream a dream
An' a wonderful wan it seem--
For I 'm off on de road I was never see,
Too long an' hard for a man lak me,
So ole he can only wait de call
Is sooner or later come to all.

De night is dark an' de portage dere
Got plaintee o' log lyin' ev'ryw'ere,
Black bush aroun' on de right an' lef,
A step from de road an' you los' you'se'f;
De moon an' de star above is gone,
Yet somet'ing tell me I mus' go on.

An' off in front of me as I go,
Light as a dreef of de fallin' snow--
Who is dat leetle boy dancin' dere
Can see hees w'ite dress an' curly hair,
An' almos' touch heem, so near to me
In an' out dere among de tree?

An' den I 'm hearin' a voice is say,
"Come along, fader, don't min' de way,
De boss on de camp he sen' for you,
So your leetle boy 's going to guide you t'roo
It 's easy for me, for de road I know,
'Cos I travel it many long year ago."

An' oh! mon Dieu! w'en he turn hees head
I 'm seein' de face of ma boy is dead--
Dead wit' de young blood in hees vein--
An' dere he 's comin' wance more again
Wit' de curly hair, an' dark-blue eye,
So lak de blue of de summer sky--

An' now no more for de road I care,
An' slippery log lyin' ev'ryw'ere--
De swamp on de valley, de mountain too
But climb it jus' as I use to do--
Don't stop on de road, for I need no res'
So long as I see de leetle w'ite dress.

An' I foller it on, an' wance in a w'ile
He turn again wit' de baby smile,
An' say, "Dear fader, I 'm here you see
We 're bote togeder, jus' you an' me--

Very dark to you, but to me it 's light,
De road we travel so far to-night.

"De boss on de camp w'ere I alway stay
Since ever de tam I was go away,
He welcome de poores' man dat call,
But love de leetle wan bes' of all,
So dat 's de reason I spik for you
An' come to-night for to bring you t'roo."

Lak de young Jesu w'en he 's here below
De face of ma leetle son look jus' so--
Den off beyon', on de bush I see
De w'ite dress fadin' among de tree--
Was it a dream I dream las' night
Is goin' away on de morning light?

Getting On

I know I 'm not too young, an' ma back is not as straight
 As it use to be some feefty year ago--
Don't care to go aroun' if de rain is fallin' down
 'Less de rheumateez is ketch me on de toe--
But dat is ma beez-nesse, an' no matter how I feel---
 Oder folk dey might look out deir own affair
'Stead o' w'isperin', "Wall! ba Gosh! lissen poor Maxime Meloche,
 How dat leetle drop o' rain is mak' heem swear!
 De ole man 's gettin' on!"

Smart folk lak dat, of course, mebbe never hear de news
    Of de tam he 's comin' sick Guillaume Laroche,
Who 's tak' heem home to die w'en de rapide's runnin' high,
    An' carry heem on hees shoulder t'roo de bush?
Oh! no, it was n't me, only wan of dem young man
    Hardly got de baby moustache on de mout',
Dat's de reason w'y I say to mese'f mos' ev'ry day,
    "Purty hard dere 's not'ing else dan talk about
    'De ole man 's gettin' on.'"

W'at 's mak' me feelin' mad is becos dey don't spik out,
    Non! dey 'll sneak aroun' for watch me as I go,
An' if I mebbe spill leetle water on de hill,
    W'en I 'm comin' from de well down dere below,
No use for tellin' me--I know too moche mese'f,
    Dat 's de tam I 'm very sure dey alway say,
"See heem now, how slow he go--don't I offen tole you so?
    We 're sorry, but Maxime is have hees day,
    De ole man's gettin' on."

It's foolish t'ing to do, for dere 's alway hang aroun'
    Some crazy feller almos' ev'ry day--
So I might a' stay at home 'stead o' tryin' feex de boom,
    Dough I 'm sure de win' is blow de oder way;
For I never hear dem shout w'en dey let de water out,
    An' de log dey come a-bangin' down de chute,
But leetle Joe Leblanc ketch me on de pant, hooraw!
    Den spile de job by w'isperin', "I 'm afraid I spik de trut',
    De ole man 's gettin' on."

Only yesterday de pig get loose an' run away,
    An' de nex' t'ing he was goin' on de corn--

So I run an' fetch de stick, an' after heem so quick
    Jus' to mak' heem feelin' sorry he was born;
An' dat pig he laugh at me, an' he fill hees belly full
    'Fore he 's makin' up his min' for come along--
I 'm sure I see heem wink--should n't wonder if he t'ink,
    "Very easy see dere 's somet'ing goin' wrong--
      De ole man 's gettin on."

If only I can get some doctor feex me up,
    Mak' me feel a leetle looser on de knee--
On de shoulder, ev'ryw'ere--ba tonder! I don't care,
    I 'le spen' a couple o' dollar, mebbe t'ree--
Jus' to larn dem feller dere how to skip an' how to jomp,
    On de way I beat deir fader long ago--
Yass siree! an' purty soon dey 'll sing anoder tune,
    An' wonder w'at de devil 's dere to show
      De ole man's gettin' on.

Oh! dat maudit rheumateez! now she's ketchin' me again
    On de back becos I 'm leetle bit excite,
An' put ma finger down, widout stoopin' on de groun'--
    But I 'll do dat trick to-morrow, not to-night--
All de sam' I often t'ink ev'ry dog is got hees day,
    Dat 's de lesson I was learnin' on de school;
So I can't help feelin' blue w'en I wonder if it 's true
    W'at dey 're sayin'--dough o' course dey 're only fool--
      De ole man 's gettin' on.

Pioneers

If dey 're walkin' on de roadside, an' dey 're bote in love togeder,
    An' de star of spring is shinin' wit' de young moon in between,
It was purty easy guessin' dey 're not talkin' of de wedder,
    W'en de boy is comin' twenty, an' de girl is jus' eighteen.

It 's a sign de winter 's over, an' it 's pleasan' hear de talkin'
    Of de bull-frog on de swamp dere wit' all hees familee--
But it 's lonesome doin' not'ing, an' dere 's not moche fun in walkin',
    So we fin' some fence dat 's handy for mese'f an' Rosalie.

An' I dunno how it happen, w'en her head come on ma shoulder,
    An' her black eye on de moonlight, lak de star shine--dat 's de way.
(Mebbe it 's becos de springtam) so I ketch her han' an' tole her
    Of how moche I 'd lak to tak' her on some contree far away.

Den she say, I 'll mak' an offer, if you 're sure you want to tak' me
    On de place I dunno w'ere--me--you mus' pay beeg price, Jo-seph.
You can carry me off to-morrow, so I 'm never comin' back--me--
    But you 'll lose upon de bargain, for de price I want 's you'se'f."

I was purty good for tradin', mebbe tak' it from ma fader,
    For de ole man 's alway tryin' show me somet'ing dat was new--
But de trade I mak' dat evenin' wit' poor Rosalie, I rader
    Not say not'ing moche about it, dough it 's bes' I never do.

So we settle on de reever wit' de bush for miles behin' us--
    Here we buil' de firse log shaintee, only me an' Rosalie--

Dat 's de woman help her husban'! an' w'en winter come an' fin' us
    We was ready waitin' for heem jus' as happy as could be.

Bar'l o' pork an' good potato, wan or two oder t'ing too
    Leetle w'isky, plaintee flour, an' wood-pile stannin' near--
Don't min' de hardes' winter, an' fat enough in spring too--
    De folk dat 's comin' handy w'en you want de contree clear!

Rosalie, you see her outside on de porch dere wit' her knittin'--
    Yass, of course I know she 's changin' since de day she marry me--
An' she 'll never sit no more dere on de fence lak leetle kitten--
    She 'd be safer on a stone wall, but she 's still ma Rosalie.

All alone: de neares' shaintee, over ten mile down de reever--
    An' might be only yesterday, I 'member it so well--
W'en I 'm comin' home wan morning affer trappin' on de beaver,
    An' ma wife is sayin', "Hurry, go an' fetch Ma-dame Labelle."

If you 're stan'in' on de bank dere, you mus' t'ink I 'm crazy feller
    By de way I work de paddle, an' de way canoe she go--
But Ma-dame know all about it, an' I never need to tell her,
    An' we jus' get back in tam' dere for welcome leetle Joe.

Dat 's de way dem woman 's doin' for help along each oder,
    For Pierre Labelle he 's comin' now an' den for Rosalie--
Of course dere 's many tam too, dey got to be godmoder--
    An' w'en dey want godfader, w'y dere 's only Pierre an' me.

Twenty year so hard we 're workin', twenty year reapin', sowin',
    Choppin' tree an' makin' portage, an' de chil'ren help us too--
But it 's never feelin' lonesome w'ile de familee is growin',
    An' de cradle seldom empty, an' we got so moche to do.

Den w'en all de work is finish, w'at dey 're callin' de surveyor
    He 's comin' here an' fin' us, an' of course so well he might--
For it 's easy job to foller, w'en de road is lyin' dere,
    So blin' man he can walk it wit' hees eyes closed, darkes' night.

An' de nex' t'ing dere 's a township, an' de township bring de taxes,
    An' it 's leetle hard on us too, dat 's way it seem to me--
An' de Gover'ment, I s'pose dey 'll never t'ink at all to ax us
    For de small account dey 're owin' mese'f an' Rosalie.

So we 'll see de beeg procession very soon come up de reever--
    Some will settle on de roadside, some will stay upon de shore--
But de ole place we be clearin', I don't t'ink we 'll never leave her,
    Dough we 're all surroun' by stranger an' we 're
    in de worl' wance more.

Natural Philosophy

Very offen I be t'inkin' of de queer folk goin' roun',
    And way dey kip a-talkin' of de hard tam get along--
May have plaintee money too, an' de healt' be good an' soun'--
    But you 'll fin' dere 's alway somet'ing goin' wrong--
'Course dere may be many reason w'y some feller ought to fret--
    But me, I 'm alway singin' de only song I know--
'T is n't long enough for music, an' so short you can't forget,
    But it drive away de lonesome, an' dis is how she go,
    "Jus' tak' your chance, an' try your luck."

Funny feller 's w'at dey call me--"so diff'ren' from de res',"
    But ev'rybody got hees fault, as far as I can see--
An' all de t'ing I 'm doin', I do it for de bes',
    Dough w'en I 'm bettin' on a race, dat 's often loss for me--
"Oho!" I say, "Alphonse ma frien', to-day is not your day,
    For more you got your money up, de less your trotter go--
But never min' an' don't lie down," dat 's w'at I alway say,
    An' sing de sam' ole song some more, mebbe a leetle slow--
    "Jus' tak' your chance, an' try your luck."

S'pose ma uncle die an' let me honder-dollar, mebbe two--
    An' I don't tak' hees advice--me--for put heem on de bank--
'Stead o' dat, some lot'rie ticket, to see w'at I can do,
    An' purty soon I 'm findin' out dey 're w'at you call de blank--
Wall! de bank she might bus' up dere--somet'ing might go wrong--
    Dem feller, w'en dey get it, mebbe skip before de night--
Can't tell--den w'ere 's your money? So I sing ma leetle song
    An' don't boder wit' de w'isky, an' again I feel all right,
    "Jus' tak' your chance, an' try your luck."

If you 're goin' to mak' de marry, kip a look out on de eye,
    But no matter how you 're careful, it was risky anyhow--
An' if you 're too unlucky, jus' remember how you try
    For gettin' dat poor woman, dough she may have got you now--
All de sam', it sometam happen dat your wife will pass away--
    No use cryin', you can't help it--dere 's your duty to you'se'f--
You don't need to ax de neighbor, dey will tell you ev'ry day
    Start again lak hones' feller, for dere's plaintee woman lef'--
    "Jus' tak' your chance, an' try your luck."

Poor man lak me, I 'm not'ing: only w'en election 's dere,
    An' ev'rybody 's waitin' to ketch you by de t'roat--
De money I be makin' den, wall! dat was mon affaire--

An' affer all w'at diff'rence how de poor man mak' de vote?
So I do ma very bes'--me--wit' de wife an' familee--
   On de church door Sunday morning, you can see us all parade--
Len' a frien' a half a dollar, an' never go on spree--
   So w'en I 'm comin' die--me--no use to be afraid--
   "Jus' tak' your chance, an' try your luck."

Champlain

"W'ere 'll we go?" says Pierre de Monts,[1]
   To hese'f as he walk de forwar' deck,
"For I got ma share of Trois Rivieres
   An' I never can lak Kebeck--
Too moche Nort' Pole--maudit! it 's cole
   Oh! la! la! de win' blow too.
An' I 'm sure w'at I say, M'sieu Pontgrave
   He know very well it 's true.

But here 's de boat, an' we 're all afloat
   A honder an' fifty ton--
An' look at de lot of man we got,
   No better beneat' de sun--
Provision, too, for all de crew
   An' pries' for to say de prayer,
So mes chers amis, dey can easy see
   De vessel mus' pass somew'ere.

If I only know de way to go

For findin' some new an' pleasan' lan',"
But jus' as he spik, he turn roun' quick,
    An' dere on de front, sir, stan' de Man.
"You was callin' me, I believe," says he,
    As brave as a lion--"Tiens!
W'en we reach de sea, an' de ship is free,
    You can talk wit' Samuel de Champlain." [2]

Wan look on hees eye an' he know for w'y
    Young Samuel spik no more,
So he shake hees han', an' say, "Young man,
    Too bad you don't come before;
But now you are here, we 'll geev' t'ree cheer,
    An' away w'erever you want to go--
For I lak your look an' swear on de Book
    You 'll fin' de good frien' on Pierre de Monts."

So de sail 's set tight, an' de win' is right,
    For it 's blowin' dem to de wes'--
An' dey say deir prayer, for God knows w'ere
    De anchor will come to res'--
Adieu to de shore dey may see no more--
    Good-bye to de song an' dance--
De girl dey love, an' de star above
    Kipin' watch on de lan' of France.

Den it 's "Come below, M'sieu Pierre de Monts,"
    Champlain he say to de capitaine--
"An' I 'll tell to you, w'at I t'ink is true
    Dough purty hard, too, for understan'--
I dream a dream an' it alway seem
    Dat God hese'f he was say to me--
'Rise up, young man, de quick you can

An' sail your ship on de western sea.

"'De way may be long, an' de win' be strong,
    An' wave sweep over de leetle boat--
But never you min', an' you 're sure to fin',
    If you trus' in me, you will kip afloat.'
An' I tak' dat ship, an' I mak' de trip
    All on de dream I was tellin' you--
An' oh! if you see w'at appear to me,
    I wonder w'at you was a-t'inkin' too?

"I come on de lan' w'ere dere 's no w'ite man--
    I come on de shore w'ere de grass is green--
An' de air is clear as de new-born year,
    An' of all I was see, dis lan's de Queen--
So I 'm satisfy if we only try
    An' fin' if dere 's anyt'ing on ma dream,
An' I 'll show de way," Champlain is say--
    Den Pierre de Monts he is answer heem,

"All right, young man, do de bes' you can--
    So long you don't bring me near Kebeck--
Or Trois Rivieres, not moche I care,
    An' I hope your dream's comin' out correc'."
So de brave Champlain he was say, "Tres bien,"
    An' soon he was boss of de ship an' crew
An' pile on de sail, wedder calm or gale--
    Oh! dat is de feller know w'at to do.

Don't I see heem dere wit' hees long black hair
    On de win' blowin' out behin'--
Watchin' de ship as she rise an' dip,
    An' always follerin' out de Sign?

An' day affer day I can hear heem say
    To de sailor man lonesome for home an' frien',
"Cheer up, mes amis, for soon you will see
    De lan' risin' up on de oder en'."

Wall! de tam go by, an' still dey cry
    "Oh! bring us back for de familee's sake."
Even Pierre de Monts fin' it leetle slow
    An' t'ink mebbe somebody mak' mistake--
But he don't geev' in for he 's boun' to win'--
    De young Champlain--an' hees heart grow strong
W'en de voice he hear say, "Never fear;
    You won't have to suffer for very long."

Alone on de bow I can see heem now
    Wan mornin' in May w'en de sun was rise--
Smellin' de air lak a bloodhoun', dere--
    An' de light of de Heaven shine on hees eyes.
A minute or more he is wait before
    He tak' off de hat an' raise hees han'--
Den down on de knee, sayin', "Dieu merci!"
    He cross hese'f dere, an' I understan'--

"Ho! Ho! De Monts! are you down below,
    Sleepin' so soun' on de bed somew'ere?
If you 're feelin' well, come up an' tell
    W'at kin' of a cloud you be seein' dere."
Den every wan shout w'en de voice ring out
    Of de young Champlain on dat summer day,
"Lan'! it is lan'!" cry de sailor man--
    You can hear dem holler ten mile away.

Port Rossignol is de place dey call

(I 'm sorry dat nam' it was disappear);
An' mos' ev'ry tree dem Frenchman see
    Got nice leetle bird singin', "Welcome here."
An' happy dey were, dem voyageurs
    An' de laugh come out on de sailors' face--
No wonder, too, w'en de shore dey view,
    For w'ere can you see it de better place?

     *   *   *   *   *   *

If you want to fin' w'at is lef' behin'
    Of de story I try very hard tell you,
Don't bodder me now or raise de row,
    But study de book de sam' I do.

[1] De-mo.

[2] Shaum-pla.

Pro Patria

Was leevin' across on de State Vermont;
    W'ere mountain so high you see--
Got plaintee to do, so all I want
    Is jus' to be quiet--me--
No bodder, no fuss, only work aroun'
    On job I don't lak refuse--

But affer de familee settle down
    It 's come w'at dey call war-news.

De Spanish da-go he was gettin' mad,
    An' he 's dangerous l'Espagnol!
An' ev'ry wan say it was lookin' bad,
    Not safe on de State at all--
So Yankee he 's tryin' for sell hees farm,
    An' town 's very moche excite,
Feexin' de gun an' de fire-alarm,
    An' ban' playin' ev'ry night.

An' soon dere 's comin', all dress to kill,
    Beeg feller from far away,
Shoutin' lak devil on top de hill,
    An' dis is de t'ing he say--

"Strike for your home an' your own contree!
Strike for your native lan'!
Kip workin' away wit' de spade an' hoe,
Den jump w'en you hear de bugle blow,
For danger 's aroun', above, below,
But de bugle will tell if it 's tam to go."

An' he tak' de flag wit' de star an' stripe,
    An' holler out--"Look at me!
If any wan touch dat flag, ba cripe!
    He 's dead about wan--two--t'ree."
Den he pull it aroun' heem few more tam,
    An' sit on de rockin' chair,
Till somebody cheer for hees Uncle Sam,
    Dough I don't see de ole man dere.

I got a long story for tell dat night
    On poor leetle Rose Elmire,
An' she say she 's sorry about de fight
    We 're doin' so well down here--
But it 's not our fault an' we can't help dat,
    De law she is made for all,
So our duty is wait for de rat-tat-tat
    Of drum an' de bugle call.

An' it 's busy week for Elmire an' me,
    I 'm sure you 'd pity us too--
Workin' so hard lak you never see,
    For dere 's plaintee o' job to do--
Den half o' de night packin' up de stuff
    We got on de small cabane--
An' buyin' a horse, dough he cos' enough,
    For Yankee 's a hard trade man.

An' how can I sleep if ma wife yell out--
    "Gedeon, dere she goes!"
An' bang an' tear all de house about
    W'en Johnnie is blow hees nose?
Poor leetle chil'ren dey suffer too,
    Lyin' upon de floor,
Wit' de bed made up, for dey never go
    On de worl' lak dat before.

We got to be ready, of course, an' wait--
    De chil'ren, de wife, an' me,
For show de Yankee upon de State,
    Ba Golly! how smart we be.
You know de game dey call checker-boar'?
    Wall! me an' ma wife Elmire,

We 're playin' dat game on de outside door
    Wit' leetle wan gader near;

Jus' as de sun on de sky go down
    An' mountain dey seem so fine,
Ev'ryt'ing quiet, don't hear a soun',
    So I 'm lookin' across de line.
An' I t'ink of de tam I be leevin' dere
    On county of Yamachiche,
De swamp on de bush w'ere I ketch de hare
    De reever I use to feesh.

An' ma wife Elmire w'en she see de tear,
    She cry leetle bit herse'f--
Put her han' on ma neck, an' say, "Ma dear,
    I 'm sorry we never lef';
But money 's good t'ing, an' dere 's nice folk too,
    Leevin' upon Vermont--
Got plaintee o' work for me an' you--
    Is dere anyt'ing more we want?

Dere 's w'at dey 're callin' de war beez-nesse--
    It 's troublesome t'ing, of course,
But no gettin' off--mus' strike wit' de res',
    No matter--it might be worse--
We 're savin' along--never lose a day,
    An' ready w'en bugle blow--"
But dat was de very las' word she say,
    For dere it commence to go,

Blowin' away on de mountain dere,
    W'ere snow very seldom melts,
Down by de reever an' ev'ryw'ere,

We could n't hear not'ing else--
Nobody stop to fin' out de place,
    Too busy for dat to-day--
But we never forget de law in de case
    W'en feller he spik dis way--

"Strike for your home an' your own contree!
Strike for your native lan'!
Kip workin' away wit' de spade an' hoe,
Den jump w'en you hear de bugle blow,
For danger 's aroun', above, below,
But de bugle will tell if it 's tam to go."

An' de chil'ren yell, an' de checker-boar'
    Don't do her no good at all--
An' nobody never jump before
    Lak de crowd w'en dey hear de call,
Dat was de familee,--bet your life
    I 'm prouder, ba Gosh! to-day
Mese'f, de leetle wan, an' de wife,
    Dan anyt'ing I can say--

'Cos nobody strike on de way we do--
    For home an' deir own contree--
Wit' fedder bed, stove, de cradle too,
    An' ev'ryt'ing else we see--
Pilin' de wagon up ten foot high
    Goin' along de road--
An' de Yankee say as we 're passin' by
    Dey never see such a load--

So dat 's how we 're comin' to Yamachiche--
    An' dat 's w'y we 're stayin' here--

Jus' to be quiet an' hunt an' feesh,
    Not'ing at all to fear--
An' if ever you lissen de Yankee folk
    Brag an' kick up de fuss--
An' say we 're lak cattle upon de yoke,
    An' away dey can trot from us--

Jus' tell dem de news of Gedeon Plouffe--
    How he jump wit' de familee
An' strike w'en de bugle is raise de roof
    For home an' hees own contree.

Getting Stout

Eighteen, an' face lak de--w'at 's de good?
    Dere 's no use tryin' explain
De way she 's lookin', dat girl Marie--
    But affer it pass, de rain,
An' sun come out of de cloud behin',
    An' laugh on de sky wance more--
Wall! dat is de way her eye it shine
    W'en she see me upon de door.

An' dere she 's workin' de ole-tam sash,

De fines' wan, too, for sure.
"Who is it for, ma belle Marie--
    You 're makin' de nice ceinture?
Come out an' sit on de shore below,
    For watchin' dem draw de net,
Ketchin' de feesh," an' she answer, "No,
    De job is n't finish yet;

"Stan' up, Narcisse, an' we 'll see de fit.
    Dat sash it was mak' for you,
For de ole wan 's gettin' on, you know,
    An' o' course it 'll never do
If de boy I marry can't go an' spen'
    W'at dey 're callin' de weddin' tour
Wit' me, for visitin' all hees frien',
    An' not have a nice ceinture."

An' den she measure dat sash on me,
    An' I fin' it so long an' wide
I pass it aroun' her, an' dere we stan',
    De two of us bote inside--
"Could n't be better, ma chere Marie,
    Dat sash it is fit so well--
It jus' suit you, an' it jus' suit me,
    An' bote togeder, ma belle."

So I wear it off on de weddin' tour
    An' long after dat also,
An' never a minute I 'm carin' how
    De win' of de winter blow--
Don't matter de cole an' frosty night--
    Don't matter de stormy day,
So long as I 'm feex up close an' tight

Wit' de ole ceinture fleche.

An' w'ere 's de woman can beat her now,
    Ma own leetle girl Marie?
For we 're marry to-day jus' feefty year
    An' never a change I see--
But wan t'ing strange, dough I try ma bes'
    For measure dat girl wance more,
She say--"Go off wit' de foolishness,
    Or pass on de outside door.

"You know well enough dat sash get tight
    Out on de snow an' wet
Drivin' along on ev'ry place,
    Den how can it fit me yet?
Shows w'at a fool you be, Narcisse,
    W'enever you go to town;
Better look out, or I call de pries'
    For makin' you stan' aroun'."

But me, I 'm sure it was never change,
    Dat sash on de feefty year--
An' I can't understan' to-day at all,
    W'at 's makin' it seem so queer--
De sash is de sam', an' woman too,
    Can't fool me, I know too well--
But woman, of course dey offen do
    Some funny t'ing--you can't tell!

Doctor Hilaire

A stranger might say if he see heem drink till he almos' fall,
"Doctor lak dat for sick folk, he 's never no use at all,"
But wait till you hear de story dey 're tellin' about heem yet,
An' see if you don't hear somet'ing, mebbe you won't forget.

Twenty odd year she 's marry, Belzemire Lafreniere,
An' oh! but she 's feelin' lonesome 'cos never a sign is dere--
Purty long tam for waitin', but poor leetle Belzemire
She 's bad enough now for pay up all of dem twenty year.

Call heem de oldes' doctor, call heem de younges' wan,
Bring dem along, no matter if ev'ry dollar 's gone--
T'ree of dem can't do not'ing, workin' for two days dere,
She was a very sick woman, Belzemire Lafreniere.

Pierre he was cryin', cryin' out on de barn behin',
Neighbors tryin' to kip heem goin' right off hees min',
W'en somebody say, "Las' winter, ma wife she is nearly go,
An' who do you t'ink is save her? ev'ry wan surely know.

"Drink? does he drink de w'isky? don't care I 'm hees only frien',
Dere 's only wan answer comin'. Wall! leetle bit now an' den
Doctor Hilaire he tak' it, but if it was me or you
Leevin' on Beausejour dere, w'at are you goin' to do?

"An' so you may t'ank de w'isky, 'cos w'ere 'll he be to-day
If he never is drinkin' not'ing? Many a mile away
Off on de great beeg city, makin' de money quick,
W'ere ev'ry wan want de doctor w'enever he 's leetle sick.

"Remember de way to get heem is tell heem it's bad, bad case,
Or Doctor Hilaire you 'll never see heem upon dis place!
Tell heem dere 's two life waitin', an' sure to be comin' die
Unless he is hurry quicker dan ever de bird can fly.

"T'orty mile crick is runnin' over de road, I 'm sure,
But if you can fin' de crossin' you 'll ketch heem at Beausejour.
Sober or drunk, no matter, bring heem along you mus',
For Doctor Hilaire 's de only man of de lot for us."

Out wit' de quickes' horse den, Ste. Genevieve has got,
An' if ever you show your paces, now is de tam to trot--
Johnnie Dufresne is drivin', w'at! never hear tell of heem,
Off on de Yankee circus, an' han'le a ten-horse team?

Dat was de lonesome journey over de mountain high,
Down w'ere de w'ite fog risin' show w'ere de swamp is lie,
An' drive as he can de faster, an' furder away he get,
Johnnie can hear dat woman closer an' closer yet.

Offen he tell about it, not'ing he never do
Geev' heem de funny feelin' Johnnie is goin' t'roo,
But he is sure of wan t'ing, if Belzemire 's comin' die,
Poor woman, she 'd never foller affer heem wit' her cry.

Dat is de t'ing is cheer heem, knowin' she is n't gone,
So he answer de voice a-callin', tellin' her to hol' on,
Till he bring her de help she 's needin' if only she wait a w'ile
Dat is de way he 's doin' all of dem t'orty mile--

Lucky he was to-night, too, for place on de crick he got,
Search on de light of day-tam, he could n't fin' better spot,
But jus' as it happen', mebbe acre or two below,

Is place w'ere de ole mail-driver 's drownin' a year ago.

W'ere is de road? he got it, an' very soon Beausejour
Off on de hillside lyin', dere she is, small an' poor,
Lookin' so lak starvation might a' been t'roo de war,
An' dere, on de bar-room sleepin', de man he is lookin' for.

Drunk? he is worse dan ever--poor leetle man! too bad!
Lissen to not'ing neider, but Johnnie is feel so glad
Ketchin' heem dere so easy, 'fore he can answer, "No"--
He 's tyin' heem on de buggy, an' off on de road he go--

Half o' de journey 's over, half o' de night is pass,
W'en Doctor Hilaire stop swearin', an' start to get quiet at las'--
Don't do any good ax Johnnie lettin' heem loose again,
For if any man tak' de chances, would n't be Johnnie Dufresne.

Hooraw for de black horse trotter! hooraw for de feller drive!
An' wan leetle cheer for Belzemire dat 's kipin' herse'f alive
Till Johnnie is bring de doctor, an' carry heem on de door
An' loosen heem out as sober as never he was before.

Quiet inside de house now, quiet de outside too,
Look at each oder smokin', dat 's about all we do;
An' jus' as we feel, ba tonder! no use, we mus' talk or die,
Dere on de house we 're hearin' poor leetle baby's cry.

Dat 's all, but enough for makin' tear comin' down de face,
An' Pierre, if you only see heem jumpin' aroun' de place
You 'd t'ink of a colt in spring-tam--den off on de barn we go
W'ere somebody got de bottle for drinkin' de healt', you know.

Takin' it too moche w'isky, is purty hard job to cure,

But only for poor ole w'isky, village of Beausejour
Can never have such a doctor, an' dat 's w'y it aint no tam
Talk very moche agin it, but fill her up jus' de sam'.

An' drink to de baby's moder, here 's to de baby too,
An' Doctor Hilaire, anoder, beeger dan all, for you.
For sober or drunk, no matter, so long as he understan'
It's very bad case is waitin', Doctor Hilaire 's de man.

Barbotte (Bull-pout)

Dere 's some lak dory, an' some lak bass,
    An' plaintee dey mus' have trout--
An' w'ite feesh too, dere 's quite a few
    Not satisfy do widout--
Very fon' of sucker some folk is, too,
    But for me, you can go an' cut
De w'ole of dem t'roo w'at you call menu,
    So long as I get barbotte--
    Ho! Ho! for me it 's de nice barbotte.

No fuss to ketch heem--no row at all,
    De sam' as you have wit' bass--
Never can tell if you hook heem well,
    An' mebbe he 's gone at las'!
An' trout, wall! any wan 's ketchin' trout
    Dey got to be purty smart--
But leetle bull-pout, don't have to look out,

For dem feller got no heart--
  Good t'ing, dey ain't got no heart

Dat 's wan of de reason I lak heem too--
  For all you have got to do
Is takin' your pole on de feeshin' hole
  An' anchor de ole canoe--
Den spit on de worm for luck, an' pass
  De leetle hook up de gut,
An' drop it down slow, jus' a minute or so,
  An' pull up de nice barbotte,
    Ha! Ha! de fine leetle fat barbotte.

Pleasan' to lissen upon de spring
  De leetle bird sing hees song,
Wile you watch de line an' look out for sign
  Of mooshrat swimmin' along;
Den tak' it easy an' smoke de pipe,
  An' w'ere is de man has got
More fun dan you on de ole canoe
  W'en dey 're bitin', de nice barbotte--
    De nice leetle fat barbotte.

No runnin' aroun' on de crick for heem,
  No jompin' upon de air,
Makin' you sweat till your shirt is wet
  An' sorry you 're comin' dere--
Foolin' away wit' de rod an' line
  Mebbe de affernoon--
For sure as he bite he 's dere all right,
  An' you 're ketchin' heem very soon--
    Yass sir! you 're gettin' heem purty soon.

Den tak' heem off home wit' a dozen more
    An' skin heem so quick you can,
Fry heem wit' lard, an' you 'll fin' it hard
    To say if dere 's on de pan
Such feesh as dat on de worl' before
    Since Adam, you know, is shut
Out of de gate w'en he 's comin' home late,
    As de nice leetle fat barbotte--
    Dat 's true, de nice leetle sweet barbotte.

THE ROSSIGNOL

Air--"Sur la Montagne"

Jus' as de sun is tryin'
    Climb on de summer sky
Two leetle bird come flyin'
    Over de mountain high--
Over de mountain, over de mountain,
Hear dem call,
Hear dem call--poor leetle rossignol!

Out of de nes' togeder,
    Broder an' sister too,
Out on de summer wedder
    W'en de w'ole worl' is new--
Over de mountain, over de mountain,

Hear dem call,
Hear dem call--poor leetle rossignol!

No leetle heart was lighter,
    No leetle bird so gay,
Never de sun look brighter
    Dan he is look to-day--
Over de mountain, over de mountain,
Hear dem call,
Hear dem call--poor leetle rossignol!

W'y are dey leave de nes' dere
    W'ere dey was still belong?
Better to stay an' res' dere
    Until de wing is strong.
Over de mountain, over de mountain,
Hear dem call,
Hear dem call--poor leetle rossignol!

W'at is dat watchin' dere now
    Up on de maple tall,
Better look out, tak' care now,
    Poor leetle rossignol,
Over de mountain, over de mountain,
Hear dem call,
Hear dem call--poor leetle rossignol!

Here dey are comin' near heem
    Singin' deir way along--
How can dey know to fear heem
    Poor leetle bird so young--
Over de mountain, over de mountain,
Hear dem call,

Hear dem call--poor leetle rossignol!

Moder won't hear you cryin',
    W'at is de use to call,
W'en he is comin' flyin'
    Quick as de star is fall?
Over de mountain, over de mountain,
Hear dem call,
Hear dem call--poor leetle rossignol?

    *   *   *   *

Up w'ere de nes' is lyin',
    High on de cedar bough,
W'ere de young hawk was cryin'
    Soon will be quiet now.
Over de mountain, over de mountain,
Hear heem call,
Hear heem call--poor leetle rossignol!

If he had only kissed her,
    Poor leetle rossignol!
But he was los' hees sister,
    An' it 's alone he call--
Over de mountain, over de mountain,
Hear heem call,
Hear heem call--poor leetle rossignol!

Only a day of gladness,
    Only a day of song,
Only a night of sadness
    Lastin' de w'ole life long.
Over de mountain, over de mountain,

Hear heem call,
Hear heem call--poor leetle rossignol!

Meb-be

A quiet boy was Joe Bedotte,
    An' no sign anyw'ere
Of anyt'ing at all he got
    Is up to ordinaire--
An' w'en de teacher tell heem go
    An' tak' a holiday,
For wake heem up, becos' he 's slow,
    Poor Joe would only say,
    "Wall! meb-be."

Don't bodder no wan on de school
    Unless dey bodder heem,
But all de scholar t'ink he 's fool
    Or walkin' on a dream--
So w'en dey 're closin' on de spring
    Of course dey 're moche surprise
Dat Joe is takin' ev'ry-t'ing
    Of w'at you call de prize.

An' den de teacher say, "Jo-seph,
    I know you 're workin' hard--

Becos' w'en I am pass mese'f
    I see you on de yard
A-splittin' wood--no doubt you stay
    An' study half de night?"
An' Joe he spik de sam' ole way
    So quiet an' polite,
    "Wall! meb-be."

Hees fader an' hees moder die
    An' lef' heem dere alone
Wit' chil'ren small enough to cry,
    An' farm all rock an' stone--
But Joe is fader, moder too,
    An' work bote day an' night
An' clear de place--dat 's w'at he do,
    An' bring dem up all right.

De Cure say, "Jo-seph, you know
    Le bon Dieu 's very good--
He feed de small bird on de snow,
    De caribou on de wood--
But you deserve some credit too--
    I spik of dis before."
So Joe he dunno w'at to do
    An' only say wance more,
    "Wall! meb-be."

An' Joe he leev' for many year
    An' helpin' ev'ry wan
Upon de parish far an' near
    Till all hees money 's gone--
An' den de Cure come again
    Wit' tear-drop on hees eye--

He know for sure poor Joe, hees frien',
    Is well prepare to die.

"Wall! Joe, de work you done will tell
    W'en you get up above--
De good God he will treat you well
    An' geev' you all hees love.
De poor an' sick down here below,
    I 'm sure dey 'll not forget,"
An' w'at you t'ink he say, poor Joe,
    Drawin' hees only breat'?
    "Wall! meb-be."

Snubbing (Tying-up) the Raft

Las' night dey 're passin', de golden plover,
    Dis mornin' I 'm seein' de bluebird's wing,
So if not'ing go wrong, de winter 's over,
    An' not very long till we got de spring.

An' nex' t'ing de reever she 'll start a-hummin',
    An' den you 'll hear it, de song an' laugh,
Is tellin' de news, de boys are comin'
    Home again on de saw-log raf'.

All very well for see dem swingin'
    Roun' de beeg islan' dere on de bay,
Nice t'ing too, for to hear dem singin',

'Cos it mak' me t'ink of de good ole day.

An' me--I could lissen dem song forever,
    But it is n't so pleasan' w'en evenin' fall,
An' dey 're lookin' for place to stay, an' never
    Snub de raf' on ma place at all---

Dat 's de fine cove if dey only know it--
    Hard to fin' better on St. Maurice,
Up de reever or down below it,
    An' house on de hill only leetle piece.

W'at is de reason den, w'en dey fin' dem
    Raf' comin' near me, dey all get scare,
An' pull lak de devil was close behin' dem,
    An' 'way down de reever to Joe Belair?

Two mile more, wit' de rock an' stone dere,
    An' water so shallow can't float canoe,
But ev'ry boy of de gang, he 's goin' dere,
    Even de cook, an' de captain too--

W'at is de reason, I lak to know--me--
    Ma own leetle cove 's lyin' empty dere,
An' nobody stop till dey go below me,
    Snubbin' de raf' on Joe Belair?

Not'ing lak dat twenty year ago, sir,
    W'en voyageurs' comin' from up above,
Dere 's only wan place us feller know, sir,
    W'en dey 're goin' ashore, an' dat's de cove.

An' dere on door of de house she 's stan'nin'

To welcome us back, Madame Baribeau,
An' Pierre hese'f, he was on de lan'nin',
    Ready for ketchin' de rope we t'row.

An' oh! de girl use to mak' us crazy--
    For many a fine girl Pierre has got--
Right on de jomp too--never lazy,
    But Sophie 's de fines' wan of de lot.

Me--I was only a comon feller,
    An' love--wall! jus' lak de leetle calf,
An' it's true, I 'm sure, w'at dey offen tell her,
    I 'm de uglies' man on boar' de raf'.

But Sophie 's so nice an' good shese'f too,
    De uglies' man upon all de worl'
Forget hees face an' forget hese'f too,
    T'ree minute affer he see dat girl--

An' dat 's de reason de chance is better,
    For you must n't be t'ink of you'se'f at all,
But t'ink of de girl if you want to get her,
    An' so we 're marry upon de fall.

An' purty soon den dey all get started,
    For marryin' fever come so strong
W'en de firse wan go, dat dey 're broken-hearted
    An' tak' mos' anyt'ing come along.

So Joe Belair, w'en hees house is buil' dere,
    He go down de reever wit' Eugenie,
An' place I settle on top de hill dere,
    De ole man geev' it to Sophie an' me.

An' along dey come, wan foller de oder,
    Dozen o' girl--not a boy at all--
Never a girl tak' affer de moder,
    But all lak de fader, beeg an' small--

A dozen o' girl, of course, no wonder
    A few of dem look lak me--sapree!
But w'en dey 're comin' dat way, ba tonder!
    She 's jus' a leetle too moche for me.

An' Joe Belair, he was down below me,
    Funny t'ing too, he is ketch also,
Ev'ryt'ing girl--how it come dunno--me--
    But dey 're all lak de familee Baribeau--

Growin' up purty de sam' de moder--
    An' soon as dey know it along de shore
De boys stop comin', an' never bodder
    For snub de raf' on ma place no more--

So w'at is de chance ma girl she 's gettin',
    Don't care w'ere I look, none at all I see,
No use, I s'pose, kipin' on a-frettin',
    Dough it's very hard case poor man lak me.

W'at 'll I do for bring dem here,--me?
    Can't be blowin' dem to de moon--
Or buil' a dam on de reever near me
    For fear we 're sure to be drownin' soon.

To-night I can hear hees darn ole fiddle,
    Playin' away on Joe Belair--

Can hear heem holler, "Pass down de middle
    An' dance on your partner over dere."

Pleasan' t'ing too, for to smell de w'isky
    Off on de leetle back room--ba oui--
Helpin' de ole folk mak' dem frisky,
    Very pleasan' for dem, but not for me--

Oh! it mak' me mad, an' I 'm tire tryin'
    To show how I feel, an' it 's hard to tell--
So I 'll geev' it up, for dere 's no good cryin';
    'Sides w'at is de use of a two-mile smell?

Non!--I don't go dere if dey all invite me,
    Or de worl' itse'f--she come to an' en'.
De Bishop hese'f, ba Gosh! can write me,
    But Jo-seph Belair, he 's no more ma frien'

Can't fin' me dere if de sky come down, sir,
    I rader ma girl she would never dance--
But far away, off on de Yankee town, sir,
    I 'll tak' dem w'ere mebbe dey have a chance.

An' reever an' cove, dough I 'll not forget dem,
    An' voyageurs too, an' Joe Belair,
Can do w'at dey lak, an' me--I 'll let dem
    Go w'ere dey want to, for I don't care.

A Rainy Day in Camp

A rainy day in camp! how you draw the blankets closer,
  As the big drops patter, patter on the shingles overhead,
How you shudder when recalling your wife's "You ought to know, sir,
  That it 's dangerous and improper to smoke a pipe in bed."

A rainy day in camp! is it possible to find better?
  Tho' the lake is like a caldron, and aloft the thunder rolls;
Yet the old canoe is safely on the shore where you can let her
  Stay as long as Jupiter Pluvius in the clouds is punching holes.

A rainy day in camp! and the latest publication
  That the mice have left unnibbled, tells you all about "Eclipse,"
How the Derby fell before him, how he beat equine creation,
  But the story yields to slumber with the pipe between your lips.

Wake again and turn the pages, where they speak of Lester Wallack
  And the heroes of the buskin over thirty years ago--
Then in case the damp surroundings cause an inconvenient colic,
  What 's the matter with the treatment neutralizing H_2O?

A rainy day in camp! what an interesting collection,
  In this magazine so ancient, of items small and great--
The History of the Negro, illustrating every section,
  So different from the present White House Colored Fashion Plate!

A rainy day in camp! and you wonder how the C. P.
  And the G. T. competition will affect the Golden West--
But these problematic matters only tend to make you sleepy,
  And again beneath the blankets, like a babe you sink to rest.

Cometh now the giant moose heads, that no eye of man can number--
 Every rain-drop on the roof-tree is a plunging three-pound trout--
Till a musk ox in a snow-drift turns and butts you out of slumber,
 And you wake to hear Bateese say, "Dat 's too bad,
 de fire 's gone out."

A rainy night in camp! with the blazing logs before us,
 Let the wolf howl in the forest and the loon scream on the lake,
Turn them loose, the wild performers of Nature's Opera Chorus
 And ask if Civilization can sweeter music make.

Josette

I see Josette on de car to-day,
 Leetle Josette Couture,
An' it 's easy tellin' she 's been away
 On market of Bonsecour--
'Cos dere 's de blueberry on de pail
 Wit' more t'ing lyin' about--
An' dere 's de basket wit' de tail
 Of de chicken stickin' out.

Ev'ry conductor along de road
 Help her de bes' he can,
An' I see dem sweat wit' de heavy load,
 Many a beeg, strong man--
But it 's differen' t'ing w'en she tak' hol',

Leavin' dem watchin' dere--
For wedder de win' blow hot or cole
   Josette never turn a hair.

Wonderful woman for seexty-five--
   Smart leetle woman sure!
An' if he 's wantin' to kip alive
   On church of de Bonsecour
De pries' he mus' rise 'fore de rooster crow,
   Or mebbe he 'll be too late
For seein' dere on de street below,
   Josette comin' in de gate.

An' half of de mornin' she don't spen' dere
   Hangin' aroun' de pew--
Bodderin' God wid de long, long prayer--
   For bote of dem got to do
Plaintee work 'fore de day's gone by,
   An' well she know--Josette--
No matter how busy an' hard she try,
   De work 's never finish yet.

An' well he know it, de habitant,
   Who is it ketch heem, w'en
He 's drivin' along from St. Laurent--
   For it 's easier bargain den--
'Cos if de habitant only sole
   De whole of hees load dat way--
Of course he 's savin' de market toll
   An' not'ing at all to pay.

Dey call her ole maid, but I can't tell--me--
   De chil'ren she has got:

No fader, no moder, dat 's way dey be--
    You never see such a lot--
An' if you ax how she fin' de clothes
    An' food for de young wan dere--
She say: "Wit' de help of God, I s'pose;
    An' de leetle shop down stair."

Comin' an' goin' mos' all de tam,
    Helpin' dem all along,
Jus' lak de ole sheep watch de lamb
    Till dey are beeg an' strong--
Not'ing lak dat I be seein' yet,
    An' it 's hard to beat for sure--
She say: "Wit' de help of God, I s'pose;
    An' de leetle shop down stair."

Comin' an' goin' mos' all de tam,
    Helpin' dem all along,
Jus' lak de ole sheep watch de lamb
    Till dey are beeg an' strong--
Not'ing lak dat I be seein' yet,
    An' it 's hard to beat for sure--
So dat 's de reason dey call Josette
    Leetle Sister of de poor.

Joe Boucher

Air--"Car si mon moine."

Joe Boucher was a frien' of mine,
    Joe Boucher was a happy man,
Till he tell a young girl he 'd lak to fin'
    Some nice leetle wife for hees new cabane.
Now he 's los' hees life too,
All on account of de wife too,
An' I know you 'll be sorry 'bout dat poor feller,
I know you 'll be sorry for Joe Boucher.

De nam' dat girl she 's Azeel-daw,
    An' purty good worker, too, dey say--
She don't lose chance for a brave garcon,
    An' so she marry Joe Boucher.
Now he 's los' hees life too,
All on account of de wife too,
An' I know you 'll be sorry 'bout dat poor feller,
I know you 'll be sorry for Joe Boucher.

Den off on de wood poor Joe he lef',
    An' w'en he 's home wit' de bird in spring,
An' fin' leetle feller jus' lak hese'f,
    Mebbe Joe don't dance an' Joe don't sing!
Now he 's los' hees life too,
All on account of hees wife too,
An' I know you 'll be sorry 'bout dat poor feller,
I know you 'll be sorry for Joe Boucher.

Dat 's all very well till de fall come along,

An' Joe got to go on de bush encore,
But w'en he come back he sing no song,
   For dere was two leetle baby more.
Now he 's los' hees life too,
All on account of de wife too,
An' I know you 'll be sorry 'bout dat poor feller,
I know you 'll be sorry for Joe Boucher.

He don't say not'ing, but he t'ink beeg lot,
   An' won't tak' a drink for two, t'ree day,
But not moche money poor Joe he got,
   So off on de reever he 's goin' away.
Now he 's los' hees life too,
All on account of de wife too,
An' I know you 'll be sorry 'bout dat poor feller,
I know you 'll be sorry for Joe Boucher.

W'en May come along dat beau garcon
   He 's only gettin' anoder scare--
For he know by de smile on Azeel-daw
   She got t'ree fine new baby dere.
Now he 's los' hees life too,
All on account of de wife too,
An' I know you 'll be sorry 'bout dat poor feller,
I know you 'll be sorry for Joe Boucher.

So he kill hese'f dead, dat beau garcon
   He work so hard for de familee,
An' he say, "Too bad, but Azeel-daw,
   I 'm sorry she marry poor man lak me."
Now he 's los' hees life too,
All on account of hees wife too,
An' I know you 'll be sorry 'bout dat poor feller,

I know you 'll be sorry for Joe Boucher.

Now I know very well dat all poor man
    He tak' some chance w'en he get marie,
So he better look out all de bes' he can,
    Or he 'll be ketch lak Joe Boucher--
Now he 's los' hees life too,
All on account of de wife too,
An' I know you 'll be sorry 'bout dat poor feller,
I know you 'll be sorry for Joe Boucher.

Charmette

Away off back on de mountain-side,
    Not easy t'ing fin' de spot,
W'ere de lake below is long an' wide,
    A nice leetle place I got,
Mebbe ten foot deep by twenty-two,
    An' if you see it, I bet
You 'll not be surprise w'en I tole to you
    I chrissen dat place Charmette.

Dat 's purty beeg word, Charmette, for go
    On poor leetle house so small,
Wit' only wan chimley, a winder or so,
    An' no galerie at all--
But I want beeg word, so de worl' will know
    W'at dat place it was mean to me,

An' dere on de book of Jean Jacques Rousseau,
    Charmette is de nam' I see.

O ma dear Charmette! an' de stove is dere,
    (Good stove) an' de wood-pile too.
An' stretch out your finger mos' anyw'ere,
    Dere 's plaintee for comfort you--
You 're hongry? wall! you got pork an' bean,
    Mak' you feel lak Edouard de King--
You 're torsty? Jus' look dere behin' de screen,
    An' mebbe you fin' somet'ing--

Ha! Ha! you got it. Ma dear Charmette.
    Dere 's many fine place, dat 's true,
If you travel aroun' de worl', but yet
    W'ere is de place lak you?
Open de door, don't kip it close--
    W'at 's air of de mornin' for?
Would you fassen de door on de win' dat blows
    Over God's own boulevard?

You see dat lake? Wall! I alway hate
    To brag--but she 's full of trout,
So full dey can't jump togeder, but wait
    An' tak' deir chance, turn about--
An' if you be campin' up dere above,
    De mountain would be so high,
Very offen de camp you 'd have to move,
    Or how can de moon pass by?

It 's wonderful place for sure, Charmette,

An' ev'ry wan say to me--
I got all de pleasure de man can get
   'Cept de wife an' de familee--
But somebody else can marry ma wife,
   Have de familee too also,
W'at more do I want, so long ma life
   Was spare to me here below?

For we can't be happier dan we been
   Over twenty year, no siree!
An' if ever de stranger come between
   De leetle Charmette an' me,
Den all I can say is, kip out de way,
   For dynamite sure I 'll get,
An' affer dat you can hunt all day
   For me an' ma dear Charmette.

Lac Souci

'Talk about lakes! dere 's none dat lies in
   Laurentide mountain or near de sea,
W'en de star 's gone off an' de sun is risin',
   Can touch w'at dey call it Lac Souci,
Restin' dere wit' de woods behin' her,
   Sleepin' dere t'roo de summer night--
But watch her affer de mornin's fin' her,
   An' over de hill-top shine de light.

See w'ere de shadder sweep de water,
    Pine tree an' cloud, how dey come an' go;
Careful now, an' you 'll see de otter
    Slidin' into de pool below--
Look at de loon w'en de breeze is ketch heem
    Shakin' hese'f as he cock de eye!
Takes a nice leetle win' to fetch heem,
    So he 's gettin' a chance to fly.

Every bird dey mus' kip behin' heem
    W'en he 's only jus' flap de wing,
Ah! dere he 's goin'--but never min' heem,
    For lissen de robin begin to sing--
Trout 's comin' up too!--dat 's beeg rise dere,
    Four of dem! Golly! it 's purty hard case,
No rod here, an' dey 're all good size dere!
    Don't ax me not'ing about de place.

No use nobody goin' murder
    T'ree an' four pounder lak dat, siree!
Wall! if you promise it won't go furder
    I 'll tole you nex' summer--bimeby--mebbe--
W'at is dat movin' among de spruce dere?
    Sure as I 'm livin' dere 's 'noder wan too--
Offen enough I 'm gettin' a moose dere,
    Non!--it 's only a couple of caribou.

Black duck so early? See how dey all come,
    Wan leetle family roun' de ben'--
Let dem enjoy it, wait till de fall come,
    Dey won't be feelin' so happy den!
Smoke on de mountain? Yass, I can smell her--
    Who is it now, Jean Bateese Boucher?

Geev' me some tam, an' I 'll feex dat feller
　　Shootin' de moose on de summer day.

W'at do you t'ink of a sapree beaver
　　Hittin' hees tail on de lake dat way?
Ought to be home wit' hees wife--not leave her
　　Workin' away on de house all day--
Funny t'ing, too, how he alway fin' me
　　Sailin' along on de ole canoe,
Lookin' for sign--den bang! behin' me
　　An' down on de water--dat's w'at he do.

Otter feeshin' an' bob cat cryin'--
　　Up on de sky de beeg black hawk--
Down on de swamp w'ere a dead log 's lyin',
　　Pa'tridge doin' hees own cake-walk!
If you never was see dem, hear dem--
　　Tak' leetle tour on de Lac Souci,
An' w'enever you 're comin' near dem,
　　You 're goin' crazy de sam' as me.

Talk about lakes of every nation,
　　Talk about water of any kin',
Don't matter you go over all creation--
　　De Lac Souci she can beat dem blin'.
Happy to leev an' happy to die dere--
　　But Heaven itself won't satisfy me,
Till I fin' leetle hole off on de sky dere
　　W'ere I can be lookin' on Lac Souci!

Poirier's Rooster

"W'at's dat? de ole man gone, you say?
    Wall! Wall! he mus' be sick,
For w'en he pass de oder day,
    He walk along widout de stick,
Lak twenty year or so--
Fine healt'y man, ole Telesphore,
I never see heem sick before,
Some rheumateez, but not'ing more--
    Please tell me how he go."

You 're right, no common t'ing for sure
    Is kill heem lak de res';
No sir! de man was voyageur
    Upon de Grande Nor' Wes'
Until he settle here
Is not de feller 's goin' die
Before he 's ready by an' bye,
So if you want de reason w'y
    I 'll tell you, never fear.

You know how moche he lak to spik
    An' tole us ev'ryt'ing about
De way de French can alway lick
    An' pull de w'ole worl' inside out,
Poor Telesphore Cadotte!
He 's knowin' all de victory,
An' braves' t'ing was never be,
To hear heem talk, it 's easy see
    He 's firse-class patriot.

Hees leetle shoe store ev'ry night
    Can hardly hol' de crowd of folk
Dat come to lissen on de fight,
    An' w'en you see de pile of smoke
An' hear ole Telesphore
Hammer de boot upon hees knee,
You t'ink of course of Chateauguay,
An' feel dat 's two, t'ree enemy
    Don't bodder us no more.

But oh! dat evening w'en he sen'
    De call aroun' for come en masse,
An' den he say, "Ma dear ole frien',
    Dere 's somet'ing funny come to pass,
I lak you all to hear--
You know dat Waterloo affair?
H-s-s-h! don't get excite, you was n't dere--
All quiet? Wall! I 'll mak' it square,
    So lissen on your ear.

"I 'm readin' on de book to-day
    (Some book, dey say, was guarantee),
An' half a dollar too I pay,
    But cheap, because it 's tellin' me
De t'ing I 'm glad to know--
Of course de w'ole worl' understan'
Napoleon fight de bes' he can,
But he 's not French at all, dat man,
    But leetle small Da-go.

"Anoder t'ing was mak' it show
    Dere 's not'ing new below de sun,

Is w'en I 'm findin' as I go--
   Dat feller dey call Welling-ton,
He 's English? No siree!
But only maudit Irlandais!
(Dat 's right! dey 're alway in de way,
Dem Irish folk), an' so I say
   I 'm satisfy for me.

"It 's not our fault, dat 's all explain--
   Dere 's no use talk of Waterloo,
Not our affair--" an' off again
   He hammer, hammer on de shoe,
An' don't say not'ing more,
But w'issle "Madame Isabeau,"
Good news lak dat is cheer heem so--
Den tak' a drink before we go,
   De poor ole Telesphore!

An' now he 's gone! Wall! I dunno,
   Can't say--he 's better off meb-be,
Don't work so hard on w'ere he go--
   Dat 's wan t'ing sure I 'm t'inkin'--me--
Unless he los' hees track.
But w'en dat boy come runnin' in
De leetle shop, an' start begin
On Poirier's rooster, how he win--
   I lak to break hees back.

Poor Telesphore was tellin' how
   Joe Monferrand can't go to sleep,
Until he 's kickin' up de row,
   Den pile dem nearly ten foot deep,
Dem English sojer man--

Can't blame de crowd dey all hooraw,
For bes' man on de Ottawaw,
An' geev' t'ree cheer for Canadaw,
   De very bes' dey can.

An' Telesphore again he start
   For tell de story leetle more,
Anoder wan before we part,
   W'en bang! a small boy t'roo de door
On w'at you call "full pelt,"
Is yellin' till it reach de skies,
"Poirier's rooster got de prize,
Poirier's rooster got de prize,
   An' win de Champion belt!"

An' sure enough, he beat dem all,
   Joe Poirier's leetle red game bird,
On beeges' show dey have dis fall,--
   De Yankee rooster only t'ird
An' Irish number two--
We hear a jump, an' Telesphore--
I never see de lak before--
He flap hees wing upon de floor
   An' cock a doodle doo!

Dat 's finish heem, he 's gone at las',
   An' never come aroun' again--
We 'll miss heem w'en we 're goin' pas',
   An' see no light upon de pane--
But pleasure we have got,
We 'll kip it on de memory yet,
An' dough of course we 'll offen fret,
Dere 's wan t'ing sure, we 'll not forget

Poor Telesphore Cadotte!

Dominique

You dunno ma leetle boy Dominique?
    Never see heem runnin' roun' about de place?
'Cos I want to get advice how to kip heem lookin' nice,
    So he won't be alway dirty on de face--
Now dat leetle boy of mine, Dominique,
    If you wash heem an' you sen' heem off to school,
But instead of goin' dere, he was playin' fox an' hare--
    Can you tell me how to stop de leetle fool?

"I 'd tak' dat leetle feller Dominique,
    An' I 'd put heem on de cellar ev'ry day,
An' for workin' out a cure, bread an' water 's very sure,
    You can bet he mak' de promise not to play!"

Dat 's very well to say, but ma leetle Dominique
    W'en de jacket we put on heem 's only new,
An' he 's goin' travel roun' on de medder up an' down,
    Wit' de strawberry on hees pocket runnin' t'roo,
An' w'en he climb de fence, see de hole upon hees pant,
    No wonder hees poor moder 's feelin' mad!
So if you ketch heem den, w'at you want to do, ma frien'?
    Tell me quickly an' before he get too bad.

"I 'd lick your leetle boy Dominique,

I 'd lick heem till he 's cryin' purty hard,
An' for fear he 's gettin' spile, I 'd geev' heem castor ile,
   An' I would n't let heem play outside de yard."

If you see ma leetle boy Dominique
   Hangin' on to poor ole "Billy" by de tail,
W'en dat horse is feelin' gay, lak I see heem yesterday,
   I s'pose you t'ink he 's safer on de jail?
W'en I 'm lightin' up de pipe on de evenin' affer work,
   An' de powder dat young rascal's puttin' in,
It was makin' such a pouf, nearly blow me t'roo de roof--
   W'at 's de way you got of showin' 't was a sin?

"Wall! I put heem on de jail right away,
   You may bet de wan is got de beeges' wall!
A honder foot or so, w'ere dey never let heem go,
   Non! I would n't kip a boy lak dat at all."

Dat 's good advice for sure, very good,
   On de cellar, bread an' water--it 'll do,
De nice sweet castor ile geev' heem ev'ry leetle w'ile,
   An' de jail to finish up wit' w'en he 's t'roo!
Ah! ma frien', you never see Dominique,
   W'en he 's lyin' dere asleep upon de bed,
If you do, you say to me, "W'at an angel he mus' be,
   An' dere can't be not'ing bad upon hees head."

Many t'ank for your advice, an' it may be good for some,
   But de reason you was geev' it is n't very hard to seek--
Yass! it 's easy seein' now w'en de talk is over, how
   You dunno ma leetle boy Dominique?

Home

"Oh! Mother the bells are ringing as never they rang before,
And banners aloft are flying, and open is every door,
While down in the streets are thousands of men I have never seen--
But friendly are all the faces--oh! Mother, what can it mean?"

"My little one," said the mother, "for many long, weary years--
Thro' days that the sunshine mocked at, and nights
    that were wet with tears,
I have waited and watched in silence, too proud to speak, and now
The pulse of my heart is leaping, for the children have kept the vow.

"And there they are coming, coming, the brothers you never knew,
But, sightless, my ears would know them, so steady and firm and true
Is the tramp of men whose fathers trod where the wind blows free,
Over the heights of Queenston, and willows of Chateaugay.

"For whether it be a thousand, or whether a single man--
In the calm of peace, or battle, since ever the race began,
No human eye has seen it--'t is an undiscovered clime,
Where the feet of my children's fathers have not stepped
    and beaten time.

"The enemy at my threshold had boasted and jeered and cried--
'The pledge of your offsprings' birthright your children
    have swept aside--
They cumber the land of strangers, they dwell in the alien's tent
Till "home" is a word forgotten, and "love" but a bow unbent.

"'Planners and builders of cities (were ever such men as these?),
Counsellors, guides, and moulders of the strangers' destinies--
Conquerors, yet are they conquered, and this is the word and sign,
You boast of their wise seed-sowing, but the harvest they reap is mine.'

"Ah! little the stranger knew me--this mocking but friendly foe,
The youngest mother of nations! how could the stranger know
The faith of the old grey mother,--her sorrows and hopes and fears?
Let her speak when her sons are tested, like mine,
 for a thousand years!

"Afar in the dim savanna when the dawn of the spring is near,
What is it wakes the wild goose, calling him loud and clear?
What is it brings him homeward, battered and tempest-torn?
Are they weaker than birds of passage, the children whom I have borne?

"Nay! the streets of the city tremble with the tread
 that shakes the world,
When the sons of the blood foregather, and
 the mother flag flies unfurled--
Brothers are welcoming brothers, and the voices that pierce the blue
Answer the enemy's taunting--and the children of York are true!

"Wanderers may be, traitors never! By the scroll
 of their fathers' lives!
The faith of the land that bore them, and the honour of their wives!
We may lose them, our own strong children, blossom and root and stem--
But the cradle will be remembered, and home is aye home to them!"

Canadian Forever

When our fathers crossed the ocean
    In the glorious days gone by,
They breathed their deep emotion
    In many a tear and sigh--
Tho' a brighter lay before them
Than the old, old land that bore them
And all the wide world knows now
    That land was Canada.

So line up and try us,
Whoever would deny us
The freedom of our birthright
    And they 'll find us like a wall--
For we are Canadian--Canadian forever,
    Canadian forever--Canadian over all.

Our fathers came to win us
    This land beyond recall--
And the same blood flows within us
    Of Briton, Celt, and Gaul--
Keep alive each glowing ember
Of our sireland, but remember
Our country is Canadian
    Whatever may befall.

So line up and try us,
Whoever would deny us
The freedom of our birthright
    And they 'll find us like a wall--

For we are Canadian, Canadian forever,
    Canadian forever---Canadian over all.

Who can blame them, who can blame us
    If we tell ourselves with pride
How a thousand years to tame us
    The foe has often tried--
And should e'er the Empire need us,
She'll require no chains to lead us,
For we are Empire's children--
    But Canadian over all.

Then line up and try us,
Whoever would deny us
The freedom of our birthright
    And they 'll find us like a wall--
For we are Canadian, Canadian forever,
    Canadian forever--Canadian over all!

Twins

I congratulate ye, Francis,
    And more power to yer wife--
An' from Montreal to Kansas,
    I could safely bet my life
Ye wor proud enough, I hould ye--
    Runnin' with the safety pins
Whin ould Mrs. Dolan tould ye,

"Milia murther! she has twins!"

Ye might kill me without warnin'--
    Lay me out there on the shelf--
For a sight of ye that mornin',
    Throwin' bookays at yerself!
Faix! ye thought ye had a cinch there,
    An' begob! so well ye might,
For not even with the Frinch there,
    Twins like thim come every night!

Francis, aisy now an' listen
    To yer mother's brother James--
Whin the twins ye go to christen,
    Don't ye give thim fancy names--
Irene--Edith--Gladys--Mavis--
    Cecil Rhodes an' Percival--
If it 's names like that, Lord save us!
    Don't live close to the canal!

Michael Whalen of St. Lambert
    Had a boy some years ago--
Called him Clarence Montizambert--
    Where he got it I dunno--
Monty used to have a brother
    (*He* was Marmaduke Fitzjames),
Killed himself some way or other
    Thryin' to pronounce his names!

Bet was three times in a minute,
    An' he thrained hard for the same,
But the lad was never in it--
    Tho' they tell me he died game!

Well, sir!--Monty grew the height of
    Fin McCool or Brian Boru--
Truth I 'm tellin', but in spite of
    Ev'rything poor Mike could do--

Divil a dacint situation
    Monty got, but dhrive a hack,
At the Bonaventure station--
    'T was the name that kept him back--
Till his friend, John Reilly, tould him,
    "Change the haythen name for Pat--"
Pathrick Joseph--now behould him
    Walkin' dillygate! think o' that!
So be careful, Master Francis,
    An' ye 'll bless yer uncle James--
Don't be takin' any chances
    With thim God-forsaken names!

Keep Out of the Weeds

No smarter man you can never know
W'en I was a boy, dan Pierre Nadeau,
An' quiet he 's too, very seldom talk,
But got an eye lak de mountain hawk,
See all aroun' heem mos' ev'ryw'ere,
An' not many folk is foolin' Pierre.

Offen I use to be t'inkin'--me--

How on de worl' it was come to be
He know so moche, w'en he never go
On college or school, ole Pierre Nadeau,
Feesh on de reever de summer t'roo,
An' trap on de winter--dat 's all he do.

"Hi! boy--Hi! put your book away,
An' come wit' your uncle Pierre to-day,
Ketch hol' of de line an' hang on tight,
An' see if your moder won't cook to-night
Some nice fresh feesh for de familee,"
Many a tam he was say to me--

An' den I 'm quiet, too scare to spik,
Wile Pierre he paddle me down de crick,
Easy an' nice he mak' her go
Close to de shore w'ere de bulrush grow,
W'ere de pike an' de beeg feesh lak to feed,
Deir nose stickin' out w'ere you see de weed--

"Lissen, ma boy," say Pierre Nadeau,
"To some of de t'ing you ought to know:
Kip a lookout on de hook an' line,
In case dey 're gettin' too far behin';
For it 's purty hard job know w'at to do,
If de reever weed 's ketchin' hol' of you.

"But if you want feesh, you mus' kip leetle close,
For dat 's w'ere de beeg feller come de mos',
Not on de middle w'ere water 's bare,
But near to de rushes over dere,
'Cos dat was de spot dey alway feed--
All de sam' you got to look out for weed.

"Ho! Ho! a strike! let heem have it now--
Gosh! ain't he a'kickin' heem up de row,
Pullin' so hard, never min', ma son,
W'en he go lak dat he was nearly done,
But he 's all right now, so don't be afraid,
Jus' hit heem again wit' de paddle blade.

"Yass! over an' over, it 's good advice,
An' me, I know, for I pay de price
On w'at you call compoun' interes' too,
For larnin' de lesson I geev' to you,
Close as you lak, but, ma boy, tak' heed
You don't run into de beeg long weed.

"An' by an' by w'en you 're growin' up,
An' mebbe drink of de black, black cup
Of trouble an' bodder an' dunno w'at,
You 'll say to you'se'f, 'Wall! I forgot
De lesson ole Pierre he know I need,'
W'en he say to me, 'Boy, look out for weed'--

"For de worl ' s de sam' as de reever dere,
Plaintee of weed lyin' ev'ryw'ere,
But work aroun' or your life is gone,
An' tak' some chance or you won't get on,
For if you don't feesh w'ere de weed is grow,
You 'll only ketch small leetle wan or so--

"Dere 's no use sayin', 'I 'll wait an' see
If some of dem feesh don't come to me,
I 'll stay outside, for it 's pleasan' here,
W'ere de water 's lookin' so nice an' clear,'

Dat 's way you 'll never get w'at you need--
Keep feeshin' away, but look out for weed."

*   *   *   *

Dat was de lesson ole Pierre Nadeau
Tell to me offen, so long ago--
Poor ole Pierre! an' I 'm tryin' too,
Tak' hees advice, for I know it 's true,
But far as it goes we 're all de same breed,
An' it 's not so easy kip out de weed.

The Holy Island

Dey call it de Holy Islan'
   W'ere de lighthouse stan' alone,
Lookin' across w'ere de breaker toss,
   Over de beeg grey stone;
Dey call it de Holy Islan,'
   For wance, on de day gone by,
A holy man from a far-off lan'
   Is leevin' dere, till he die.

Down from de ole, ole people,
   Scatter upon de shore,
De story come of Fader Jerome,

De pries' of Salvador
Makin' hees leetle house dere,
    Wit' only hees own two han',
Workin' along, an' singin' de song
    Nobody understan'.

"All for de ship an' sailor
    Out on de stormy sea,
I mak' ma home," say Fader Jerome,
    "W'ere de rock an' de beeg wave be
De good God up on de Heaven
    Is answer me on de prayer,
An' bring me here, so I 'll never fear,
    But foller heem ev'ryw'ere!"

Lonely it was, dat islan',
    Seven league from de coas',
An' only de cry, so loud an' high,
    Of de poor drown sailors' ghos'
You hear, wit' de screamin' sea gull;
    But de man of God he go
An' anchor dere, an' say hees prayer
    For ev'rywan here below.

Night on de ocean 's fallin',
    Deep is de fog, an' black,
As on dey come, to deir islan' home,
    De sea-bird hurryin' back;
W'at is it mak' dem double
    An' stop for a minute dere,
As if in fear of a soun' dey hear,
    Meetin' dem on de air?

Sweeter dey never lissen,
    Magic it seem to be,
Hangin' aroun', dat wonderful soun',
    Callin' across de sea;
Music of bell 's widin it,
    An' foller it on dey go
High on de air, till de islan' dere
    Of Salvador lie below.

Dat 's w'ere de bell 's a-ringin'
    Over de ocean track,
Troo fog an' rain an' hurricane,
    An' w'enever de night is black;
Kipin' de vow he 's makin',
    Dat 's w'at he 's workin' for,
Ringin de bell, an' he do it well,
    De Fader of Salvador!

An' de years go by, an' quickly,
    An' many a sailor's wife
She 's prayin' long, an' she 's prayin' strong
    Dat God he will spare de life
Of de good, de holy Fader,
    Off w'ere de breakers roar,
Only de sea for hees companie,
    Alone on Salvador.

    *   *   *   *

Summer upon de islan',
    Quiet de sea an' air,
But no bell ring, an' de small bird sing,
    For summer is ev'ryw'ere;

A ship comin' in, an' on it
   De wickedes' capitaine
Was never sail on de storm, or gale,
   From here to de worl's en'!

"Geev' me dat bell a-ringin'
   For not'ing at all, mon pere;
Can't sleep at night, w'en de moon is bright,
   For noise she was makin' dere.
I'm sure she was never chrissen,
   An' we want no heretic bell;
W'ere is de book? For you mus' look
   An' see if I chrissen it well!"

Leevin' heem broken-hearted,
   For Fader Jerome is done,
He sail away wit' de bell dat day,
   Capitaine Malcouronne;
An' down w'ere dead man 's lyin',
   Down on de ocean deep,
He sink it dere, w'ile he curse an' swear,
   An' tole it to go to sleep.

An' t'ree more year is passin',
   An' now it 's a winter night:
Poor Salvador, so bles' before,
   Is sittin' among de fight
Of breaker, an' sea-bird yellin',
   An' noise of a tousan' gun,
W'en troo de fog, lak a dreefin' log,
   Come Capitaine Malcouronne!

Gropin' along de sea dere,

Wonderin' w'ere he be,
Prayin' out loud, before all de crowd
   Of sailor man on hees knee;
Callin' upon de devil,
    "Help! or I 'm gone!" he shout;
"Dat bell it go to you down below,
   So now you can ring me out

"To de open sea, an' affer
   I promise you w'at I do,
Yass, ev'ry day I 'll alway pray
   'To you, an' to only you--
Kip me in here no longer,
   Or de shore I won't see again!"
T'ink of de prayer he 's makin' dere,
   Dat wicked ole capitaine!

An' bell it commence a-ringin',
   Quiet at firse, an' den
Lak tonder crash, de ship go smash,
   An' w'ere is de capitaine?
An' de bell kip ringin', ringin',
   Drownin' de breakers' roar,
An' dere she lie, w'ile de sea-birds cry,
   On de rock of Salvador.

The Riviere des Prairies

I see de many reever on de State an' ev'ryw'ere,
    From Maine to California, New York to Michigan,
An' wan way an' de oder, I tell you I don't care;
    I travel far upon dem as moche as any man--
But all de t'ousan' reever I was never pass along,
    For w'at dey call de beauty, from de mountain to de sea,
Dere 's wan dat I be t'inkin,' de wan w'ere I belong,
    Can beat dem all, an' easy, too, de Riviere des Prairies!

Jus' tak' de Hudson Reever, an' de Mississippi too,
    Missouri, an' de res' of dem, an' oders I can't t'ink,
Dey 're all beeg, dirty places, wit' de steamboat gruntin' troo,
    An' de water runnin' in dem is black as any ink,
An' de noises of dem reever never stoppin' night or day,
    An' de row along de shore, too, enough to mak' you scare;
Not a feesh is wort' de eatin', 'less you 're starvin by de way,
    An' you 're feeling purty t'orsty if you drink de water dere!

So ketch de han' I geev' you w'ile I 'm on de humor now,
    An' I bet you won't be sorry w'en you go along wit' me,
For I show you all aroun' dere, until you 're knowin' how
    I come so moche to brag--me--on de Riviere des Prairies.
It 's a cole October mornin', an' de maple leaf is change
    Ev'ry color you can t'ink of, from de purple to de green;
On de shore de crowd of blackbird, an' de crow begin' arrange
    For de journey dey be takin' w'en de nort' win's blowin' keen.

Quick! down among de bushes!--don't you hear de wil' goose cry
    An' de honk de great beeg gander he was makin' up above?
On de lake dey call Two Mountain is de place dey 're goin' fly,

But only spen' de night-tam, for dey 're alway on de move;
Jus' see de shadder dancin' up an' down, up an' down,
    You t'ink dem geese was passin' in an' out between de tree
W'en de branch is bendin' over on de water all aroun'
    Now you see de place I 'm talkin', dat 's de Riviere des Prairies!

Missouri! Mississippi! better wait till you go back--
    No tam for talk about dem w'en dis reever you can see,
But watch de cloud a-sailin' lak a racer on de track,
    An' lissen to de music of de Riviere des Prairies--
An' up along de shore dere, don't you envy Bord a Plouffe?
    Oh! dat's de place is lucky, have de reever come so near--
I 'm knowin' all de people, ev'ry chimley, ev'ry roof,
    For Bord a Plouffe she never change on over feefty year!

St. Martin's bell is ringin', can't you hear it easy now?
    Dey 're marryin' or buryin' some good ole frien' of me,
I wonder who it can be, don't matter anyhow,
    So long as we 're a-lookin' on de Riviere des Prairies.
Only notice how de sun shine w'en he's comin' out to peep,
    I 'm sure he 's leetle brighter dan anyw'ere you see,
An' w'en de fall is over, an' de reever 's gone to sleep,
    De w'ites' snow is fallin' on de Riviere des Prairies!

I love you, dear ole reever, more dan ev'ry Yankee wan;
    An' if I get de money, you will see me on de train,
Wit' couple o' t'ousan' dollar, den hooraw! it 's goodbye, John!
    You can kill me if you ketch me leavin' Bord a Plouffe again.
But sometam it 'll happen dat a feller 's gettin' stop
    Because he's comin' busy wit' de wife an' familee--
No matter, if de good God he won't forget to drop,
    Ev'ry day an' night, hees blessin' on de Riviere des Prairies!

The Wind that Lifts the Fog

Over de sea de schooner boat
Star of de Sout' is all afloat,
Many a fine brave feesherman
Sailin' away for Newfunlan';
Ev'ry feller from St. Malo,
Dem is de boy can mak' her go!
Tearin' along t'roo storm or gale,
Never sparin' an inch of sail--

Down below w'en de night is come,
Out wit' de bottle an' t'ink of home,
Push it aroun' till bottle 's drain,
An' drink no more till we 're home again,
"Here 's to de win' dat lif' de fog,
    No matter how she 's blowin',
Nort' or sout', eas' or wes',
Dat is de win' we love de bes',
Ev'ry sailor an' young sea dog,
Here 's to de win' dat lif' de fog
    An' set de ship a-goin'."

Flyin' over de wave she go,
Star of de Sout' from St. Malo,
Never a tack, before she ran
Out on de bank of Newfunlan'--
Drop de anchor, an' let her down,
Plaintee of comrade all aroun',
Feeshin' away till night is fall,

Singin' away wit' ev'ry haul,
"Here 's to de win' dat lif' de fog,
No matter how she 's blowin',
Nort' or sout', eas' or wes',
Dat is de win' we love de bes',
Ev'ry sailor an' young sea dog,
Here 's to de win' dat lif' de fog
An' set de ship a-goin'."

      *   *   *   *

Star of de Sout'--did you see de light
Steamin' along dat foggy night?
Poor leetle bird! anoder star
Shinin' above so high an' far
Dazzle you den, an' blin' de eye,
Wile down below on de sea you lie
Anchor dere--wit' your broken wing
How could you fly w'en de sailor sing
"Here 's to de win' dat lif' de fog
No matter how she 's blowin',
Nort' or sout', eas' or wes',
Dat is de win' we love de bes',
Ev'ry sailor an' young sea dog,
Here 's to de win' dat lif' de fog
An' set de ship a-goin'"?

The Fox Hunt

I'm all bus' up, for a mont' or two,
　　On account of de wife I got,
Wit' de fuss an' troublesome t'ing she do,
　　She 's makin' me sick a lot;
An' I 'm sorry dat woman was go to school
　　For larnin' de way to read,
Her fader an' moder is great beeg fool
　　For geevin' her more she need!

'Cos now it 's a paper ev'ry week,
　　Dollar a year, no less--
Plaintee o' talkin' about musique,
　　An' tell you de way to dress;
Of course dat 's makin' her try to sing
　　An' dress, till it 's easy see
She 's goin' crazy about de t'ing
　　Dey 're callin'--Societee.

Las' week, no sooner I come along
　　From market of Bonsecour,
Dan I 'm seein' right off, dere 's somet'ing wrong,
　　For she 's stannin' outside de door
Smilin' so sweetly upon de face,
　　Lookin' so nice an' gay--
Anywan t'ink it 's purty sure case
　　She marry me yesterday.

Can't wait a minute till supper's t'roo
　　Before she commence to go--

"Oh! Johnnie, dere 's somet'ing I mus' tole you--
    Somet'ing you lak to know--
To-morrow we 're goin' for drive aroun'
    An' it won't be de heavy load,
Jus' me an' you, for to see dem houn'
    T'row off on de Bord a Plouffe road."

"Denise, if dat was de grande affaire
    On w'at you call a la mode--
Lookin' dem fox dog stannin' dere
    T'row off on de Bord a Plouffe road,
You can count me out!" An' she start to cry--
    "You know very well," she say,
"I don't mean dat--may I never die
    But you 're a beeg fool to-day!

"Johnnie, to-morrow you 'll come wit' me
    Watchin' dem run de race,
Ketchin' de fox--if you don't, you see
    We 're bote on de beeg disgrace.
Dey 're all comin' out from de reever side,
    An' over from Beaurepaire,
Seein' de folk from de city ride,
    An' ev'rywan 's sure be dere."

All right--an' to-morrow dere's two new shoe,
    So de leetle horse mak' de show,
Out wit' de buggy: de new wan too,
    Only get her ten year ago--
An' dere on de road, you should see de gang
    Of folk from aroun' de place,
Billy Dufresne, an' ole Champagne,
    Comin' to see de race,

Wit' plaintee of stranger I never see,
    An' some of dem from Pointe Claire,
All of dem bringin' de familee,
    W'enever dere 's room to spare.
Wonderful sight--I 'm sure you say--
    To see how Societee
(W'atever dat mean?) she got de way
    Of foolin' de w'ole contree.

Den I 'm heetchin' de horse on de fence, for fear
    Somebody run away,
So man wit' de bugle he 's comin' near,
    An' dis is de t'ing he say--
"You see any fox to-day, ma frien',
    Runnin' aroun' at all,
You know any place he got hees den?
    For we lak it to mak' de call."

An' me--I tell heem, "You mus' be wrong,
    An' surely don't want to kill
De leetle red fox, about two foot long,
    Dat 's leevin' below de hill;
Jompin' de horse till he break hees knee,
    Wile spotty dog mak' de row,
For a five-dollar fox? You can't fool me--
    I know w'at you 're wantin' now!

"You hear de story of ole Belair,
    He 's seein' de silver fox
W'enever he 's feeshin' de reever dere,
    Sneakin' along de rocks."
But ma wife get madder I never see,

An' say, "Wall! you *mus'* be green--
Shut up right away," she 's tellin' me,
   "It 's de leetle red fox he mean!"

So me--I say not'ing, but watch de fun---
   An' spotty dog smell aroun'
Till dey start to yell, an' quick as a gun
   Ev'rywan 's yellin', "Foun'!"
An' de way dey 're goin' across de fiel',
   De lady in front, before,
Dunno, but I 'm willin' to bet good deal
   Somebody mus' be sore!

Over de fence dey 're jompin' now,
   Too busy for see de gate
Stannin' wide open, an' den dey plough
   Along at a terrible rate;
All for de small red fox, dey say,
   Only de leetle fox,
You 're buyin' for five dollar any day,
   An' put heem on two-foot box.

I 'm foolish enough, but not lak dat--
   Never lak dat at all,
Sam' as you see a crazy cat
   Tryin' to climb de wall;
So I say to ma wife, I 'm satisfy
   On ev'ryt'ing I was see,
But happy an' glad, until I die,
   I 'm not on Societee!

Losin' a day on de fall 's no joke,
   Dat 's w'at I 'm tellin' you,

Jus' for de pleasure of see dem folk
    Dress up on de howdy do;
So I 'm sorry you go to school,
    Larnin' de readin' dere--
Could do it mese'f, an' play de fool,
    If money I got to spare.

But potatoes a dollar a bag,
    An' easy to sell de load,
Watchin' de houn' to see heem wag
    Hees tail, on de Bord a Plouffe road
Foolin' away w'en de market 's good
    For seein' Societee
Chasin' de leetle fox t'roo de wood
    Wit' crazy folk!--no siree!

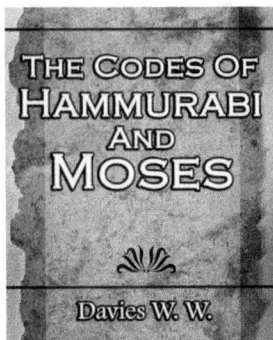

The Codes Of Hammurabi And Moses
W. W. Davies

QTY

The discovery of the Hammurabi Code is one of the greatest achievements of archaeology, and is of paramount interest, not only to the student of the Bible, but also to all those interested in ancient history...

Religion ISBN: *1-59462-338-4* Pages:132

MSRP $12.95

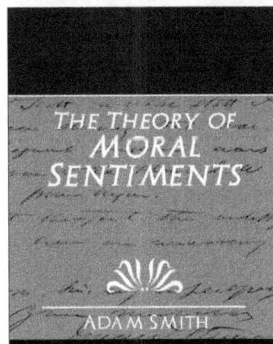

The Theory of Moral Sentiments
Adam Smith

QTY

This work from 1749. contains original theories of conscience amd moral judgment and it is the foundation for systemof morals.

Philosophy ISBN: *1-59462-777-0* Pages:536

MSRP $19.95

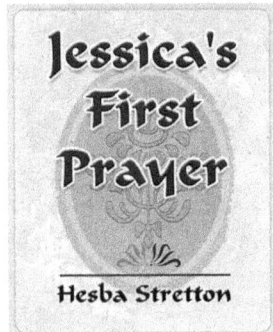

Jessica's First Prayer
Hesba Stretton

QTY

In a screened and secluded corner of one of the many railway-bridges which span the streets of London there could be seen a few years ago, from five o'clock every morning until half past eight, a tidily set-out coffee-stall, consisting of a trestle and board, upon which stood two large tin cans, with a small fire of charcoal burning under each so as to keep the coffee boiling during the early hours of the morning when the work-people were thronging into the city on their way to their daily toil...

Pages:84

Childrens ISBN: *1-59462-373-2* *MSRP $9.95*

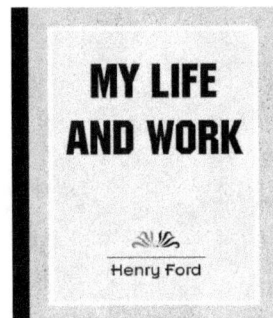

My Life and Work
Henry Ford

QTY

Henry Ford revolutionized the world with his implementation of mass production for the Model T automobile. Gain valuable business insight into his life and work with his own auto-biography... "We have only started on our development of our country we have not as yet, with all our talk of wonderful progress, done more than scratch the surface. The progress has been wonderful enough but..."

Pages:300

Biographies/ ISBN: *1-59462-198-5* *MSRP $21.95*

www.bookjungle.com *email: sales@bookjungle.com fax: 630-214-0564 mail: Book Jungle PO Box 2226 Champaign, IL 61825*

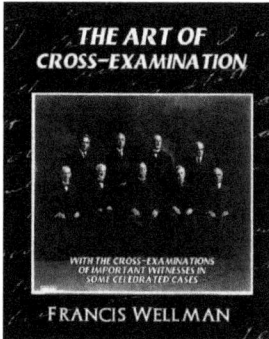

The Art of Cross-Examination
Francis Wellman

QTY

I presume it is the experience of every author, after his first book is published upon an important subject, to be almost overwhelmed with a wealth of ideas and illustrations which could readily have been included in his book, and which to his own mind, at least, seem to make a second edition inevitable. Such certainly was the case with me; and when the first edition had reached its sixth impression in five months, I rejoiced to learn that it seemed to my publishers that the book had met with a sufficiently favorable reception to justify a second and considerably enlarged edition. ...

Reference   ISBN: *1-59462-647-2*

Pages:412
MSRP $19.95

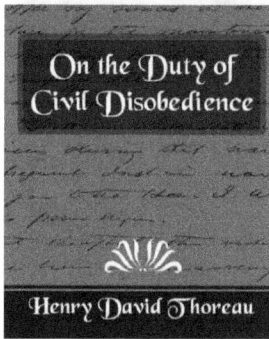

On the Duty of Civil Disobedience
Henry David Thoreau

QTY

Thoreau wrote his famous essay, On the Duty of Civil Disobedience, as a protest against an unjust but popular war and the immoral but popular institution of slave-owning. He did more than write—he declined to pay his taxes, and was hauled off to gaol in consequence. Who can say how much this refusal of his hastened the end of the war and of slavery ?

Law   ISBN: *1-59462-747-9*

Pages:48
MSRP $7.45

Dream Psychology Psychoanalysis for Beginners
Sigmund Freud

QTY

Sigmund Freud, born Sigismund Schlomo Freud (May 6, 1856 - September 23, 1939), was a Jewish-Austrian neurologist and psychiatrist who co-founded the psychoanalytic school of psychology. Freud is best known for his theories of the unconscious mind, especially involving the mechanism of repression; his redefinition of sexual desire as mobile and directed towards a wide variety of objects; and his therapeutic techniques, especially his understanding of transference in the therapeutic relationship and the presumed value of dreams as sources of insight into unconscious desires.

Psychology   ISBN: *1-59462-905-6*

Pages:196
MSRP $15.45

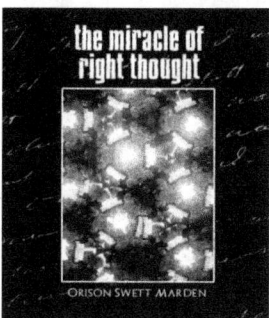

The Miracle of Right Thought
Orison Swett Marden

QTY

Believe with all of your heart that you will do what you were made to do. When the mind has once formed the habit of holding cheerful, happy, prosperous pictures, it will not be easy to form the opposite habit. It does not matter how improbable or how far away this realization may see, or how dark the prospects may be, if we visualize them as best we can, as vividly as possible, hold tenaciously to them and vigorously struggle to attain them, they will gradually become actualized, realized in the life. But a desire, a longing without endeavor, a yearning abandoned or held indifferently will vanish without realization.

Self Help   ISBN: *1-59462-644-8*

Pages:360
MSRP $25.45

QTY

The Rosicrucian Cosmo-Conception Mystic Christianity *by Max Heindel*　　ISBN: *1-59462-188-8*　**$38.95**
The Rosicrucian Cosmo-conception is not dogmatic, neither does it appeal to any other authority than the reason of the student. It is: not controversial, but is: sent forth in the, hope that it may help to clear...　　*New Age/Religion Pages 646*

Abandonment To Divine Providence *by Jean-Pierre de Caussade*　　ISBN: *1-59462-228-0*　**$25.95**
"The Rev. Jean Pierre de Caussade was one of the most remarkable spiritual writers of the Society of Jesus in France in the 18th Century. His death took place at Toulouse in 1751. His works have gone through many editions and have been republished...　　*Inspirational/Religion Pages 400*

Mental Chemistry *by Charles Haanel*　　ISBN: *1-59462-192-6*　**$23.95**
Mental Chemistry allows the change of material conditions by combining and appropriately utilizing the power of the mind. Much like applied chemistry creates something new and unique out of careful combinations of chemicals the mastery of mental chemistry...　　*New Age Pages 354*

The Letters of Robert Browning and Elizabeth Barret Barrett 1845-1846 vol II　　ISBN: *1-59462-193-4*　**$35.95**
by Robert Browning and Elizabeth Barrett　　*Biographies Pages 596*

Gleanings In Genesis (volume I) *by Arthur W. Pink*　　ISBN: *1-59462-130-6*　**$27.45**
Appropriately has Genesis been termed "the seed plot of the Bible" for in it we have, in germ form, almost all of the great doctrines which are afterwards fully developed in the books of Scripture which follow...　　*Religion/Inspirational Pages 420*

The Master Key *by L. W. de Laurence*　　ISBN: *1-59462-001-6*　**$30.95**
In no branch of human knowledge has there been a more lively increase of the spirit of research during the past few years than in the study of Psychology, Concentration and Mental Discipline. The requests for authentic lessons in Thought Control, Mental Discipline and...　　*New Age/Business Pages 422*

The Lesser Key Of Solomon Goetia *by L. W. de Laurence*　　ISBN: *1-59462-092-X*　**$9.95**
This translation of the first book of the "Lemegton" which is now for the first time made accessible to students of Talismanic Magic was done, after careful collation and edition, from numerous Ancient Manuscripts in Hebrew, Latin, and French...　　*New Age/Occult Pages 92*

Rubaiyat Of Omar Khayyam *by Edward Fitzgerald*　　ISBN:*1-59462-332-5*　**$13.95**
Edward Fitzgerald, whom the world has already learned, in spite of his own efforts to remain within the shadow of anonymity, to look upon as one of the rarest poets of the century, was born at Bredfield, in Suffolk, on the 31st of March, 1809. He was the third son of John Purcell...　　*Music Pages 172*

Ancient Law *by Henry Maine*　　ISBN: *1-59462-128-4*　**$29.95**
The chief object of the following pages is to indicate some of the earliest ideas of mankind, as they are reflected in Ancient Law, and to point out the relation of those ideas to modern thought.　　*Religiom/History Pages 452*

Far-Away Stories *by William J. Locke*　　ISBN: *1-59462-129-2*　**$19.45**
"Good wine needs no bush, but a collection of mixed vintages does. And this book is just such a collection. Some of the stories I do not want to remain buried for ever in the museum files of dead magazine-numbers an author's not unpardonable vanity..."　　*Fiction Pages 272*

Life of David Crockett *by David Crockett*　　ISBN: *1-59462-250-7*　**$27.45**
"Colonel David Crockett was one of the most remarkable men of the times in which he lived. Born in humble life, but gifted with a strong will, an indomitable courage, and unremitting perseverance...　　*Biographies/New Age Pages 424*

Lip-Reading *by Edward Nitchie*　　ISBN: *1-59462-206-X*　**$25.95**
Edward B. Nitchie, founder of the New York School for the Hard of Hearing, now the Nitchie School of Lip-Reading, Inc, wrote "LIP-READING Principles and Practice". The development and perfecting of this meritorious work on lip-reading was an undertaking...　　*How-to Pages 400*

A Handbook of Suggestive Therapeutics, Applied Hypnotism, Psychic Science　　ISBN: *1-59462-214-0*　**$24.95**
by Henry Munro　　*Health/New Age/Health/Self-help Pages 376*

A Doll's House: and Two Other Plays *by Henrik Ibsen*　　ISBN: *1-59462-112-8*　**$19.95**
Henrik Ibsen created this classic when in revolutionary 1848 Rome. Introducing some striking concepts in playwriting for the realist genre, this play has been studied the world over.　　*Fiction/Classics/Plays 308*

The Light of Asia *by sir Edwin Arnold*　　ISBN: *1-59462-204-3*　**$13.95**
In this poetic masterpiece, Edwin Arnold describes the life and teachings of Buddha. The man who was to become known as Buddha to the world was born as Prince Gautama of India but he rejected the worldly riches and abandoned the reigns of power when... Religion/History/Biographies Pages 170

The Complete Works of Guy de Maupassant *by Guy de Maupassant*　　ISBN: *1-59462-157-8*　**$16.95**
"For days and days, nights and nights, I had dreamed of that first kiss which was to consecrate our engagement, and I knew not on what spot I should put my lips..."　　*Fiction/Classics Pages 240*

The Art of Cross-Examination *by Francis L. Wellman*　　ISBN: *1-59462-309-0*　**$26.95**
Written by a renowned trial lawyer, Wellman imparts his experience and uses case studies to explain how to use psychology to extract desired information through questioning.　　*How-to/Science/Reference Pages 408*

Answered or Unanswered? *by Louisa Vaughan*　　ISBN: *1-59462-248-5*　**$10.95**
Miracles of Faith in China　　*Religion Pages 112*

The Edinburgh Lectures on Mental Science (1909) *by Thomas*　　ISBN: *1-59462-008-3*　**$11.95**
This book contains the substance of a course of lectures recently given by the writer in the Queen Street Hail, Edinburgh. Its purpose is to indicate the Natural Principles governing the relation between Mental Action and Material Conditions...　　*New Age/Psychology Pages 148*

Ayesha *by H. Rider Haggard*　　ISBN: *1-59462-301-5*　**$24.95**
Verily and indeed it is the unexpected that happens! Probably if there was one person upon the earth from whom the Editor of this, and of a certain previous history, did not expect to hear again...　　*Classics Pages 380*

Ayala's Angel *by Anthony Trollope*　　ISBN: *1-59462-352-X*　**$29.95**
The two girls were both pretty, but Lucy who was twenty-one who supposed to be simple and comparatively unattractive, whereas Ayala was credited, as her Bombwhat romantic name might show, with poetic charm and a taste for romance. Ayala when her father died was nineteen...　　*Fiction Pages 484*

The American Commonwealth *by James Bryce*　　ISBN: *1-59462-286-8*　**$34.45**
An interpretation of American democratic political theory. It examines political mechanics and society from the perspective of Scotsman James Bryce　　*Politics Pages 572*

Stories of the Pilgrims *by Margaret P. Pumphrey*　　ISBN: *1-59462-116-0*　**$17.95**
This book explores pilgrims religious oppression in England as well as their escape to Holland and eventual crossing to America on the Mayflower, and their early days in New England...　　*History Pages 268*

www.bookjungle.com *email: sales@bookjungle.com fax: 630-214-0564 mail: Book Jungle PO Box 2226 Champaign, IL 61825*

QTY

The Fasting Cure *by Sinclair Upton*   ISBN: *1-59462-222-1*   **$13.95**

In the Cosmopolitan Magazine for May, 1910, and in the Contemporary Review (London) for April, 1910, I published an article dealing with my experiences in fasting. I have written a great many magazine articles, but never one which attracted so much attention... New Age/Self Help/Health Pages 164

Hebrew Astrology *by Sepharial*   ISBN: *1-59462-308-2*   **$13.45**

In these days of advanced thinking it is a matter of common observation that we have left many of the old landmarks behind and that we are now pressing forward to greater heights and to a wider horizon than that which represented the mind-content of our progenitors... Astrology Pages 144

Thought Vibration or The Law of Attraction in the Thought World   ISBN: *1-59462-127-6*   **$12.95**

by William Walker Atkinson   Psychology/Religion Pages 144

Optimism *by Helen Keller*   ISBN: *1-59462-108-X*   **$15.95**

Helen Keller was blind, deaf, and mute since 19 months old, yet famously learned how to overcome these handicaps, communicate with the world, and spread her lectures promoting optimism. An inspiring read for everyone... Biographies/Inspirational Pages 84

Sara Crewe *by Frances Burnett*   ISBN: *1-59462-360-0*   **$9.45**

In the first place, Miss Minchin lived in London. Her home was a large, dull, tall one, in a large, dull square, where all the houses were alike, and all the sparrows were alike, and where all the door-knockers made the same heavy sound... Childrens/Classic Pages 88

The Autobiography of Benjamin Franklin *by Benjamin Franklin*   ISBN: *1-59462-135-7*   **$24.95**

The Autobiography of Benjamin Franklin has probably been more extensively read than any other American historical work, and no other book of its kind has had such ups and downs of fortune. Franklin lived for many years in England, where he was agent... Biographies/History Pages 332

Name	
Email	
Telephone	
Address	
City, State ZIP	

☐ **Credit Card**   ☐ **Check / Money Order**

Credit Card Number	
Expiration Date	
Signature	

Please Mail to: *Book Jungle*
PO Box 2226
Champaign, IL 61825
or Fax to: *630-214-0564*

ORDERING INFORMATION

web: *www.bookjungle.com*
email: *sales@bookjungle.com*
fax: *630-214-0564*
mail: *Book Jungle PO Box 2226 Champaign, IL 61825*
or PayPal *to sales@bookjungle.com*

Please contact us for bulk discounts

DIRECT-ORDER TERMS

**20% Discount if You Order
Two or More Books**
Free Domestic Shipping!
Accepted: Master Card, Visa,
Discover, American Express